Badass Grandma Chronicles
One Woman's Journey
Volume 1
Written by Sandra Allensworth

Copyright © 2025 by Sandra Allensworth All Rights Reserved.
Cover Art and Illustrations: Cheryl Poindexter
GENERAL DISCLAIMER: The names and photos were changed to protect the guilty, innocent, and unskilled.
NO AI TRAINING: Without in any way limiting the author's and publisher's exclusive rights under copyright, any use of this publication to "train" generative artificial intelligence (AI) technologies to generate text is expressly prohibited. The author reserves all rights to license use of this work for generative AI training and development of machine learning language models.

ISBN:
Paperback 979-8-9876758-6-1
E-Book 979-8-9876758-7-8

Dedication

This book is dedicated to my grandchildren and great grandchildren who call me GrandSandra. It is a title I wear with honor. As one of them told me from the wisdom of his six years: "Your name is GrandSandra because you are so Grand!"

I wish that it were so.

Table of Contents

1. The Repossession
2. Gathering Longhorns
3. The Naked Man
4. Fighting the Snake
5. Stringing Hot Wire
6. The Air Balloon
7. Moving the House
8. Saving the Well Driller's Equipment
9. The Traffic Stop
10. Vandalism and the Hustle
11. Latifa, Bubba and Rowena
12. The Squatter
13. Tracking the Bull
14. The Story of Daft
15. Accused of Kidnapping
16. Sue Happy Sara
17. The Bicyclist
18. Southern Engineering
19. The Air Show
20. Lulu the Laundress
21. Agnes
22. Betty and Rodger
23. The Hole That Did Not Swallow the House
24. The Tornado
25. Goldenrod and the Cows
26. Another Mad Cow
27. The Black Panther
28. The Sewer Line
29. The Witch and the Curse
30. Lolli's Story

Chapter 1
The Repossession

One Mother's Day my daughter called me and asked where I was. I told her I was in Texas. She asked me what I was doing. I told her I was repossessing a car. The owner of a car dealership had asked his brother to go to Texas and pick up some parts for a car wash and while he was there to look for a car that he had financed. The people had left the state without paying and gone to Friona, Texas, or so he had heard.

Brother Dell and I went to Friona, and we drove up and down some streets and then Dell said that he was not going to look any more and was going to the 7-11 to go to the bathroom and then we would leave town. I was willing to continue looking, but Dell said that we needed to get the parts picked up and further searching would be useless.

We pulled into the station and while he went to the men's room, I strolled around the tiny grocery store. I noticed a small group of teenagers talking in a group. I eased up to the young people and asked them, with a smile, "Do you all live around here?" They said that they did, so I said, "I have a friend, Sara, that I haven't seen in a long time.

Someone told me that she might live around here. I heard she got married so I don't know her last name. The last time I saw her she drove a blue 1988 Chevy. Has anyone seen her around here?"

The kids were oh-so-helpful. They gave me directions to her house, carefully explaining that the trailer sat back off the road, and you could not see it until you got right up on it.

When Dell exited the bathroom, I whispered to him to get in the truck, quickly, that I had found something.

We drove right up to the house and the man who had skipped the state without paying for the car was removing things from the vehicle. When he looked up and saw the dealership truck, his shoulders dropped. Busted!

Dell handed me his pistol and told me to stay in the truck unless things went sideways. He stepped out of the flatbed truck and, in a very polite manner, began talking to the man. I watched as the thief got all his possessions out of the car and Dell signaled for me to come get in the car. I drove it off to a neutral location. Dell followed me in the dealer truck. We loaded it on the flatbed and went to find the needed parts.

When we got back to the auto dealership, Dell's brother was delighted that we had found the $10,000 dollar car. This was in the 1990s. In 2025 dollars that would have been $25,000. He told me when I needed a vehicle to let him know. About a year later he gave me a good deal on a beautiful, blue, 1996 GMC that I drove until the drunk hit me.

Chapter 2
Gathering Longhorns

For many years I had a boyfriend named Walt. He was a rancher. His father was an old-time cow and horse trader. One day Walt said that his dad, Mason, had gotten word of two longhorns which had been jumping the fence and getting out on the highway about 80 miles away near a National Park. They were 12-year-old steers. Some other cowboys had tried to catch them and had given up. They had grown increasingly wild and cagey as numerous cowboys had chased and harassed them.

Because they kept getting on the highway, orders had been given for the steers to be shot, as a public safety measure. Mason convinced the powers-that-be to let him have a try at catching the steers before they were put down. Walt, his sister and her two kids, Mason, Johnny (a local ranch hand) and I headed south to try to do what others had failed to accomplish. Walt had a good horse, but Johnny's horse was green.

We parked two pickups with cattle trailers in the middle of the pasture. Johnny and Walt unloaded their horses. Mason stayed with one truck and Walt's sister and two girls, and I stood in the bed of the other truck so we could see what was going on.

The men chased those steers into and out of gullies, through cactus and across flatland. The steers would lie down to hide and then come up fighting. At one point one of the steers hid in a deep gully and when Walt chased him out, the steer bolted up and over the lip of the gully, with his six-foot-wide horns, straight into the path of Johnny and his green broke horse. His horse's eyes got very wide, so that the whites showed. He jumped sideways and when Johnny tried to control him, he broke in two. He started bucking hard and was rendered useless for the chase. Walt finally wore the steer down. He and Johnny roped and loaded him into one trailer with Mason's help. Sister and her kids and I watched from the second pickup.

Walt and Johnny searched for a long time for the second steer until the only place left to look was a grove of trees. Walt tied his horse and Johnny stayed horseback while Walt went into the trees, afoot, searching. The steer bolted from the trees and Johnny cut him off. Walt jumped on his horse and took off after him. It was beautiful to behold to see Walt riding hard, build a huge loop, and then see it settle over the head and one horn. He later said that he would have had to tie two ropes together to catch both horns. LOL.

Roping requires two hands and a horse that is as dedicated to the task as the rider. Walt dallied. That means that he wrapped the end of the rope around the saddle horn, fully committing to the struggle. That is a tricky maneuver because leaving too much slack between your hands can cost you a thumb when the animal hits the end of the rope. As Walt stood far off the saddle to the left, trying to gain leverage and keep from getting pulled over by the steer, the animal headed towards the bed of the truck that Sister, the kids and I were standing in. When it looked like he was going to join us, Sister and the kids bailed off the right side.

I stood firm, but moved to the center of the bed, near the cab. The steer headed for the truck, pulling Walt and the horse

behind him. Walt reined his horse to a different angle as he and his horse strained to gain control.

I wasn't about to lose my bird's eye view of the action. The steer and I were eyeball to eyeball, a few feet apart. I still remember those eyes. They did not look like cow eyes to me. They reminded me of the shark eyes in Jaws. I jumped and spread my arms wide to get his attention. I thought if he saw me in the truck, he would not climb in. It would have been a wreck if he had. Not that I was stupid. I would have jumped off the other side, if necessary.

The steer turned away and Walt finally jerked him down. He was standing in the saddle, and it was twisted sideways on the horse, as they leaned against the weight of the steer. He yelled at his dad to bring the trailer. The steer lay there, either having given up or resting for another fight. Mason brought the trailer alongside the steer and opened the gate. I jumped down to help. Walt ran the rope through the trailer and put a loop around one of the side rails. He then handed me the rope to use as a pulley and we inched that huge steer into the trailer. He had to turn his head sideways to get inside.

A few days later Walt and I branded them. They never even flinched when those hot irons burned their hides. Mason sold them to an attorney in another town for a tourist attraction. I was so glad that I got to witness some very real cowboying that day. I still have some pictures of those steers and a great memory.

Chapter 3
The Naked Man

I bought a large bull calf, uncut. He weighed around 700 pounds. He was a crossbred dairy calf so he would not be of any use as a bull. I bought him cheap and thought that once I castrated him that he would be worth much more as a steer since he would gain more weight. So goes my thinking.

There was a large irrigation canal behind my house, mostly lined with trees. The embankment was probably six feet higher than the land where my house and my neighbor's house were located. A dirt road followed the water. The ditch riders used it to check on the irrigation gates and the amount of water being used.

My neighbors, Henry and Carla, lived south of me, just before the bend of the canal. Like my house, it was nestled under a few trees.

I got up early one morning and went to feed the steer. GONE. Oh, crap! I looked around and saw that he was up on the canal road.

I climbed over the barbed wire fence and fell in behind the steer, strategizing. At the end of my property was a short road leading down off the embankment. It was my sincere hope that by going slowly, I could get the steer to turn down that road instead of continuing straight on the canal road. If he kept on the canal road, it would mean that he could get into the cemetery or go further on, and with a right turn get on the main road leading to the highway or by turning left, head straight into town. No good would come from any of those decisions.

Did he make the turn? Nope! Straight past the turn off and still cruising down the canal road. He had his eye on me and only walked fast enough to maintain the distance. I ever so slowly closed the distance between us. As I got even with Henry and Carla's house, I noticed that Henry was standing in the yard, buck-naked, hosing off with a water hose. I don't know why. Didn't they have running water? Was he too dirty to shower in the house? Was someone using the shower? Maybe he just liked showering al fresco. It was a beautiful morning.

Quick thinking me. I knelt with my face turned away from him and pretended to be tying my shoe. In a loud voice, I chastised the bull, calling him names and telling him how stupid he was and what I was going to do to him when I caught him. I only hoped that Henry would hear me. I stood up and continued to follow the bull around the bend in the canal.

At this point the bull bolted and kicking his heels in the air, ran down the embankment into a field of weeds. I hurried forward on the road so I could get in front of him. This was my chance to head him off. I did it! Then I slid down the embankment to redirect the errant bovine in the right direction. He dodged past me and ran back up the embankment- but heading home.

Again, I fell in behind him, slowly, so as not to give him any reason to change directions. We made it down to the bend in the canal. So far, so good. We were coming close to Henry's barn. I thought this would probably be a good barrier. If I could get him past the barn, he should head straight home. Wrong again. He barreled off the canal road and ran kicking, farting and snorting around Henry's barn.

As I jumped and slid down the embankment, I looked up and there went Henry, running as only a buck-naked bank auditor could run, heading for his house. The steer was fast on his heels. It was a sight to behold. A naked man, knees pumping faster than he was moving forward, headed for his back door. I assume that his method of running was because he was barefoot, and the ground was rocky.

I didn't want Henry to think that I saw him, so I scrambled back up the embankment and ran past the barn hoping to catch up with the steer. When I got past the barn, I jumped and slid down the embankment again, until I came face to face with Carla, wrapped in a fluffy, pale pink bathrobe, holding a large glass of iced tea and staring stony faced, intently into my eyes.

"Oh! Hi Carla. My bull got out and I've been chasing him. Have you seen him?"

"He's behind the barn."

"I'm so sorry! I just got him. As soon as I castrate him, I'll take him to the pasture. I hope he didn't hurt anything."

"No."

"Is it OK if I go get him?'

She nodded stiffly and watched me intently as I started after the bull. That was the end of our conversation. I don't know if I was convincing, but I will never forget the sight of that naked bank auditor, with knees pumping high, hot footing it to his back door and my half-grown bull, snorting and farting, fast on his heels.

Chapter 4
Fighting The Snake

One year when the grass was scarce, I had trouble finding any pasture for my cattle. The only place available was a long, skinny strip of land that ran along the river. Every morning, before daylight, I started work rebuilding the fence. It was laid completely over, probably since no one had removed the tumbleweeds which stacked up against the fence, creating a wind barrier. This allowed the wind to push over the fence for about a mile or so along the road.

At the time I was sharing a pasture with a man who was real long on talk and real short on work. I'll call him Billy. He never could get out to the pasture to do any fence building. To keep the cattle off the river and keep them from crossing over to the neighbor's pasture, we decided to lay miles of black plastic pipe from the one watering tank which had a tank that pumped water from the river to a tank in another pasture.

I purchased the pipe, knowing that I would have to figure out how to get Billy's half of the money from him later in the season. Billy met me at the pasture, and we started by hooking up the pipe to the tank. We then started unrolling the pipe which came in very heavy rolls about 6 feet tall. We slowly backed across the pasture going around cactus and brush, strategizing over the easiest way to go across gullies. Slowly we made our way across the first pasture and under the first fence. Then across the second pasture and under the fence, on our way to another tank.

We suddenly started hearing the familiar sound of rattlesnakes and froze. Turning slowly around to locate the direction of the sound, we found two snakes, male and female entwined, wrapped in close embrace, working on making little rattlesnakes. As we approached, they separated. When I later told that story, I always said that we found them lying side by side smoking tiny cigarettes. LOL.

A note of curiosity here. I did not know that snakes have genitalia on each side of their nether regions. Since they breed by wrapping around each other, I guess this guarantees that no matter which way they twist, whether they are left-handed or right-handed, they are bound to get the job done.

Anyway, Billy said he would go get his gun. Since that meant a run across two pastures, it pretty much guaranteed that he would miss all the action. My truck was one pasture closer, since I had the rolls of pipe, so I ran and got my shovel and ran back to do battle. My personal attitude is that the only good snake is a dead snake.

The female got away, but the male and I did battle. I won.

I cut off his head. By this time, Billy was back with his trusty pistol. He set it down, took my shovel and buried the head. The fangs were still capable of poisoning anything they touched.

Being polite, I asked Billy if he wanted the snake. He did not. I did. I took the headless snake home and put him in my freezer. My intention was to either make a belt or at the very least a hat band for my grey Stetson. The only way that I knew to tan a snake hide was to soak it in antifreeze for a period of time.

Because I worked so many hours, I didn't want to take a chance of my dogs getting into the antifreeze. That is a very slow, painful way for a dog to die. That is why the snake ended up in my freezer.

When the grandkids came to see me, they always asked to "pet the snake."

No, I never got that snake tanned. When I finally moved, a few years later, I disposed of the rattler. I cut the rattles off first and gave them to a grandson for show and tell. So, the brave old snake came to an ignominious end.

Chapter 5
Stringing Hotwire in the Snow

I was running cattle on the Pecos River. The man running his cattle across the river would not do his part to keep up the fences. I'll call him Dick. Since I worked full time and he had hired hands, the whole labor division seemed a little one sided.

In fact, he was trying to make it hard for me to keep my cattle in. He wanted me to quit ranching and vacate the property. He had offered to lease the property I was on, but the owner of the property was a friend and my champion. My champion I will call Arthur, as in King Arthur. Champion of the underdog.

I was out at daylight every morning before going to my day job, taking care of the cattle and fixing any fence or water tank that needed my attention. Dick and his friends could be found at the café drinking coffee and shooting the bull. I found out that Dick had complained to Arthur about my cattle getting onto his land. Arthur got mad and told him, "Don't come to me complaining. While you all sit here on your butts, that poor woman is out there working her tail off, taking care of business." While I appreciated his sentiments, his words did not endear me to Dick and his friends.

When the cattle got onto his pasture one time, he had his hired hands, on horseback, gather my cattle and drive them into a pen on his side of the river. He then called the brand inspector who chewed me out and threatened to confiscate them. It would have been faster and easier, not to mention being a better neighbor, to have the men find the place where the fence was down and fix it or find the gate and push the cattle back onto my pasture. There is no end to low end.

Anyway, it snowed. And it snowed. And it snowed. There was about two feet of very wet snow. I decided the fastest thing to do, since I couldn't find the gap, was to put up hot wire around the smaller pasture until the weather cleared.

I hired a man, Enrique, who spoke very little English, to help me. I loaded my horse and supplies and met him at the river. My plan, as I gestured to him, was for me to ride with a bucket of four-foot rebar stakes tied to my saddle and drop them every eight feet around the pasture and then go back and take a wheel of smooth wire and unstring it next to the posts. Enrique's job was to drive the posts into the ground and put the plastic connectors on the stakes and then string the wire onto the stakes. It seemed like a solid plan. It was cold.

The mare, Enrique and I worked along most of the day and got the wire up. My cattle respected the fence because I always put short flags of yellow caution tape on the wire. Because they spin in the wind the cattle would stick their noses on them out of curiosity. Since they were standing in wet snow, they would get a serious shock when their noses touched the wire. So far so good. I hooked up the fence to the battery charger and we walked through the snow for a ways testing to be sure that the charge was good, all the way around the pasture. I had, however, forgotten to bring any tools other than a pair of pliers with me.

The way you test if a wire is hot is this—You touch one end of a metal tool to the metal post and then touch another end of the tool close to the wire, thereby making a connection. I normally have a screwdriver for this task. If you come close to the wire with the other end of the tool, a spark will jump between the two metal pieces proving a connection.

I can only say that I was very tired and very cold and therefore my brain was shutting down. I touched one part of the pliers to the post and then very carefully moved the other half of the pliers toward the wire. I mistakenly thought that the plastic cover on the handles of the pair of pliers would insulate me from a shock. I was very wrong.

My boots were wet, my jeans were wet, I was standing in wet snow, and I wanted so much to go home and get dry and warm.

The jolt that went through me hit my heart like the kick of a horse. I jumped and shouted, reflexively.

Enrique stood a few feet from me and when I jumped, I looked at him. His eyes were huge, his face was ashen, his mouth was open, but no words came out. We had no common words to express anything, but he started chattering something in Spanish. When I caught my breath and my heart quit fibrillating, I said the only thing I could think of in Spanish. "Vamanos." We gathered everything and he walked while I rode. I paid him and he left. My heart hurt all night, but I was fine. If I ever need electric paddles administered, I think I will know how they feel.

When the snow melted and I could finally ride the fence, I found the spot where the cattle went through. It was in the bend of the river where the fence stopped, right at the edge of a bluff, which plunged down to the river. The fence was down for about five feet before the drop off. It is a wonder that I ever found it.

Chapter 6
The Air Balloon

I did a lot of volunteer work after my family grew up. At one point I oversaw the VIP tents at the local air show. As a thank you, one of the board members invited all of those who made the air show possible to a breakfast and a balloon ride. Wahoo!

A great breakfast and a chance to socialize with like-minded people. Banana Fosters for dessert. Then we gathered at the launch field. The wind needs to be reasonably still for the balloon to fly. Many a balloon fiesta has been cancelled due to high wind conditions.

The sound of the balloon filling with hot air? Well, kind of like a strong wind in a long tunnel, or the crash of an angry ocean, or the roar of a lion from deep in a cave. Anyway, you get the idea. The balloon slowly filled with hot air from the propane ignited fire and large fans which pushed the hot air into the deflated monster. It lifted like a reincarnated beast rising from the dead. Three people at a time got in the basket with the pilot. It gently ascended and drifted off to the south.

Because many people were waiting to ride, the balloon was not deflated, so as each ride ended, the balloon gently touched down. Those who had followed the balloon took their turns as the crew held the balloon in place while each contingent of riders exited the gondola (basket) and others took their places. I stood back and watched. The friends of the pilot and the breakfast host took the first rides. The morning progressed and the wind started to pick up.

Finally, there was only me and an older woman, Mrs. Aston, left waiting for our turn. Mike announced that the wind was getting up and this would be the last ride for the day and the ride might get bumpy. That was not going to stop me or Mrs. Aston. We entered the basket, and Mike turned the burners up, allowing us to rise.

We scudded across the sky much faster than the normal 10 mph or so that you usually see. Usually, a balloon drifts with the wind. Our flight was progressing much more briskly. Finally, we got out of town and headed toward the airfield of the abandoned air base.

We watched the chase crew as it kept an eye on us and calculated the direction we would take. It was obvious that Mike was struggling to keep the balloon off the ground but beneath the high winds that had suddenly come up, as he looked for a place to safely set down. It was exhilarating to watch the dogs going crazy, barking and spinning around, as we whizzed by overhead. One large brown dog broke out of the backyard and took off down the road. We skimmed the treetops so close that I could almost reach out and touch the leaves.

It is amazing how clearly you can hear the conversations coming from the ground. There was no conversation in the basket until Mike spoke up. "We are going to have to cut this trip short. The winds are getting up."

I watched Mike fiddling with the levers, trying to adjust for speed and altitude. There was a look of deep concentration on his weatherbeaten face. He finally spoke again. "We have to set down. Quickly. We have a choice of trying to clear that fence ahead of us or set down hard before we get to it. The problem with trying to get over the fence is that we might hit it." The commercial height chain link fence loomed ahead, and we were fast approaching it. I don't know how tall it was, but it served as a barrier to our landing.

Mike made the call. "Ladies, we are going to have a hard landing. I am going to hold Mrs. Aston on my lap. Sandra, you take hold of the cables on either side of you and hang on tight." With that, Mike squatted in the basket with the frail Mrs. Aston on his lap and I hung on for my dear and precious life. The balloon hit hard but did not tip over. It bounced once and was still. Whew! That was exhilarating!

Chasing balloons is half the fun. You have to drive on the roads and keep an eye on the balloon to be at the proper location when it touches down. The lucky ones get to grab hold of the basket and hold it while the massive balloon deflates. Then fold up the balloon. If you ever get a chance to go to a balloon fiesta, go. If you are invited to be part of a chase crew, say yes. If you get a chance to ride in a balloon?

Chapter 7
Moving the House

It took several years for me to dig myself out of the hole my ex had dug for us. I got the kids and the debts. He took everything else. He was averse to work. I hadn't seen him in a year and a half, but he still got half of my six-month-old calves, two pickups and I can't remember what else. I told him to take what he wanted and that it would have been cheap at twice the price to get rid of him. I had to refinance the mobile home again to clear the notes on the pickups. My banker told me that I didn't have to do that. I did it anyway. That is how I arrived at a place where I could buy another home to put on my property.

I went to Albuquerque to look at doublewides. Waaay too much money. For several years I had driven by a property in Roswell where a house mover had stored all the nice older houses for sale. He had purchased them from the El Paso Natural Gas Pipeline. In years past, the company had built communities of houses around their stations. The compressor, dehydration and purification plant at Jal, New Mexico was built in 1947. In the late 1980's, the Company auctioned off the houses and they were moved around the country.

Royal bought several and moved them to Roswell. I watched the houses disappear from the property over several months. I had my eye on a three bedroom. Financing was not available for buying and moving a house. Hence my dilemma. I finally decided to sell some of my heifers to facilitate the purchase. That hurt because I was trying desperately to build a herd of mother cows. By the time I got everything gathered up, there was only one two bedroom left.

By this time, Royal had gone to work for a house mover out of town. He made arrangements for another mover, Bert, to relocate my house for me. He also arranged for his employer to finance the house for five years once I got it situated. That would give me time to remodel the house so that I could get a permanent loan on the house and property. The garage and laundry room were not moved with the house, leaving open walls. Also, no back door. Don't care, I took it.

Bert went to my property, moved my single wide trailer into the middle of a field and scraped off a place for the house.

When the day came for the move, I was a couple of miles away getting drinking water. My well water was so bad that it left a white film on everything. I was filling water jugs at a faucet set up by the Cotton Gin a few miles from my property and looked up in time to see my house go by, hooked on a truck. It is hard to explain how I felt. My heart started to pound, and I started crying. I had spent so many years struggling to get my children raised, get everything paid off and then to get someone to finance my endeavor, and then come up with the money to pay for the move. It was very emotional to me. Finally, my own house, a real house, was on its way to my property. I jumped in my pickup and pulled in behind my home as it went by.

We got to the turn off and the first obstacle presented itself. The driver and assistant were consulting on the best way to get past the large trees which overhung the road. Burt must have seen me but pretended that he did not. The overhanging porch is what presented the problem. He put his hand over one eye and spoke.

"I think if we just close one eye and keep going, we might make it. OH! Wait! Here's the boss, I guess we can't do that."

I didn't think that was funny.

"Royal didn't tell me about this when he asked for a price to move this house."

I didn't think that was very funny either.

The assistant got on top of the house with a long pole and lifted the branches up and on top of the house, as Burt slowly inched forward. I knew as I watched the branches drug across the shingles that I would have to replace them. No problem, I could do that. I kept thinking that I wonder what they would have done if I had not been there. Knowing his reputation, I suspect he would have charged through the trees and then claimed that the house came that way.

The next obstacle soon presented itself. There were two power poles across and slightly staggered from each other. If they had been exactly across from each other, the house would not have fit between them. I had to admire what he did. He aimed the truck slightly to the right and inched forward, toward the irrigation ditch. Clearing the porch, he then cut back sharply to the left and managed to get past the power pole on the left. At no time was there more than about two inches between either of them or my house. He did it! Yah!

The next obstacle was the corner at the end of my property. There was a concrete irrigation ditch on both sides of the narrow road and no way to maneuver around the corner. I told the guys that I could go around the section and come into my property from the other side. I had several railroad cross ties at the corrals. They waited while I loaded up the cross ties and I brought them to them.

After filling in the ditch with the cross ties, and taking down my fence, they were able to ease over the ditch very slowly and finally get the house on my property. Whew!

The next obstacle was trickier. Burt got out and did a lot of measuring and figuring. In a few days some men came out and laid three layers of cinder block to serve as the footing for my new domicile. He set up the footing of cinder blocks, three high, leaving room for the metal beams which were used as a sling to move the house. I lived in the trailer in the middle of the field for a few weeks without running water or electricity. I strung an extension cord out to the trailer and lived there. I could have a light bulb or a tv. Things were sparse, but worth it.

He left me sitting in the field like that for several weeks until I made a call to Royal and insisted that they finish setting up my house. In a few days, here came the men. I was in the house when they showed up and began to winch the house over the blocks. As they got ready to set it down, Burt stuck his head in the front door and said, "You are going to have to sit still while we drop this thing." The house was lifted with a crane boom. The long arm of the boom pulled the cables up. They were attached to either end of the beams with the house sitting on top of the beams. I sat, leaning against a wall, holding my breath while they gently lowered the house onto its permanent foundation. "Thank you, Lord!!!"

I climbed out of the house to survey the accomplishment. Absolutely beautiful. There were shingles below the floor line of the house, and they had set the house down with a half inch gap on either side. They did not break one shingle. Incredible!

Making it livable is a story for another time. But this was MINE!. Home at last.

Chapter 8
Saving the Well Driller's Equipment

Before I tell this story, I want to write a little eulogy to the lowly Fence Pliers. This one tool takes the place of a pair of regular pliers, a screwdriver, a hammer, a wire cutter and a pry bar. It fits in your back pocket. I am on my third pair. I prefer a not-new pair because you can hold one leg of the pliers in your hand with only your thumb and let the other leg fall open, ready for work. They saved my hand one time when the barbed wire snapped and curled around my hand. I was able to cut myself loose.

Fence Pliers are normally 10 inches long. Where the two legs come together, they slightly swell. They taper down together and then flare at the bottom, covered in a plastic coating. This prevents them from slipping out of your grip. At the crotch where they pivot is a set of ridges on each side that serve as a crimper or wire grip. On both sides of the head there are two small blades that will cut a barb wire. The head on one side comes to a beak on the outside to pry with.

The outside of the other side has a flat head with ridges which serve as a hammer. The corrugation prevents it from slipping off of whatever you are hammering. The inside of the two halves come together like a bird's beak. They can pinch and pull a staple or nail. The top of the two sides forms a curve which serves as a lever to pry out the staple or stretch a wire. God bless the man who invented this tool!

And so on with the story. It was Saturday. I was at the river, putting up a fence in this new location, in order to move my cattle off the ranch, which had been sold. The property I was working on had not been used for years. I had to clean out places for the cattle to water and put up the four strand barbed wire fence that had laid completely over. When tumbleweeds and such blow against a fence, if you don't remove them, they will form a wind break and eventually push the fence over. This is especially true in the sandy soil by the river.

This early Saturday morning I had flipped a mile of fence over so I could reach the fence staples and pull them out. This would also leave everything on the right side of the fence line when I resurrected it. I heard a tractor at work about two miles up the road. The well driller, Rufus, who had bought the property, was across the road with a tractor, clearing an area to start drilling a well. There was a small house a few hundred feet north and a larger home a few hundred feet south of the work area. Neither of the renters were home. I could see the well drilling truck parked next to a flatbed with several canisters of something.

The morning went by. It was past noon. It was getting hot. I looked up and saw smoke rising. I continued working and occasionally checked on the smoke. It was getting darker and starting to billow, rising high in the sky. Apparently, I was the only one in the valley this morning.

I became concerned, so I drove to the work area. There was a grass fire surrounding the truck, getting closer and closer. I stepped into the smoke and started yelling for Rufus and his helper. I couldn't believe that no one was left to watch the equipment.

I looked in the truck to make sure that no one was inside then called 911 for the fire department. Then I called the only café in town. Rufus wasn't there, neither was his helper. The fire call was relayed to Artesia, about 50 miles away. The dispatcher then called the volunteer fire department, which was about 25 miles from the fire. Then I grabbed my shovel. I began by shoveling dirt on the fire which was licking at the tires of the truck. Then I started shoveling dirt on the pool of oil that was on fire beneath the tractor. It had a small leak, and the fire was licking up the drips falling from the crankcase. Then I stopped the fire from getting to the flatbed with the tanks of whatever fuel he was using. Probably for welding.

When all the fire was smothered, I leaned against my tailgate catching my breath and watching for any flames that might erupt, so I could put them out. Wondering where in the hell was the fire truck.

Finally!! I could see an ancient firetruck rumbling over the hill. The men spilled out of the truck and began tossing dirt on the hot spots. About that time a woman who lived in the larger house drove up. She got out of the Suburban and threw herself on the hood of the car, screaming and weeping, flailing her arms. Very dramatic. I said to her, "Really? The fire is out. It didn't get to your house." The volunteer fire chief patted me on a shoulder and said, "You are a Wonder Woman. Thank God you were here. When we got the call, they said that it was a grass fire. We didn't want to bring our new fire truck to a grassfire. This old clunker only goes about 25 miles an hour, that's why it took so long. Rufus owes you a big one."

I heard from others that Rufus told people that every time he saw me after that, that he wanted to kiss me. Two truck tires had to be replaced but his truck, well drilling equipment, the tractor and trailer were saved. I don't recall that he ever thanked me. Maybe he did. It would have been nice if he had ever offered to buy me a cup of coffee.

Chapter 9
The Traffic Stop

For a few years I owned a Brown Diesel Toyota pickup. People teased me about the horse trailer that pushed it around the countryside.

I still had one child at home. Her last year of high school. We got dressed up to go to the Lyn Larson Organ Concert. We were dressed in our finest and smelled wonderful. We left the house and drove twenty-three miles to Roswell.

As we approached the city limits, I noticed that a police officer had pulled over a black Toyota. The officer's head swiveled and followed me as I drove past. I whizzed on by at the posted speed limit. Within a block, that police car flashed his lights, and I pulled over, convinced of my innocence.

I watched as the officer cautiously got out of his car and approached. He had his hand on his pistol and sidled up alongside my truck. I put both of my hands in my lap and patiently waited. He ever so slowly peered around the corner of the pickup until he was looking at me, and then my daughter. In hindsight I should have had my hands on the steering wheel, but I didn't know that, then. He had a look of shocked surprise when he finally came face to face with me as our perfume wafted out the window and he saw two nicely dressed females sitting in the truck. He very sternly asked for my identification. I complied. I asked why I was being stopped, and he ignored the question. He told me to stay in the truck. I watched as he went back to his patrol car and got on the radio. I waited an inordinate amount of time while he sat in the squad car.

He finally got out and put his foot on my back bumper and started writing down things. Again, I waited. This should not have been taking so long.

I finally got out to see what was going on. I tend to confront things head on. He said that this truck matched the description of a truck that was involved in the armed robbery of a convenience store the week before. I assured him that this was not the truck since it never left my possession, and I was not responsible for the theft.

I volunteered this piece of information. About a week before I was awakened in the middle of the night by flashing lights and several sheriff's cars in my front yard. The dog was upset. I went out in time to see one officer put his hand on the hood of my truck and then walk back to the group. They apparently wanted to be sure that it had not been driven lately. I asked them what was going on and they said that there was nothing going on and left. The only one left was our local constable who told me the story.

Someone in a brown Toyota had robbed a convenience store in Roswell and was chased to our little burg. The thief had apparently ditched the officers by turning around and heading back to town. The deputies asked the constable if there was anyone with a brown Toyota in town. He mentioned me and Floyd.

Floyd owned a brown Toyota pickup. It was not a diesel pick up. The tailgate was a lever action instead of a pull action, as was mine. Other than that, the two were identical. Floyd was a small-time outlaw. I was not.

They couldn't find Floyd, but the constable told them that I would not have been involved. The deputies insisted on coming to my house and checking on this. I related this story to the officer who stopped me on my way to the concert. He listened and then said, "Maybe you should sell this truck."

They later caught Floyd, and he was in and out of trouble all the time until he finally ended up in prison. I kept the truck for years because of the good gas mileage.

Chapter 10
Vandalism and the Hustle

I was working on a rental one day when a young man knocked on the door. My assistant answered the door, and the visitor asked to pick pecans from the tree in the back yard. Manuel called for me to come to the door. The visitor was wearing a long jacket that I call a shoplifter's jacket because it has a large trapezoidal shape with deep pockets. It also has a hoodie which, when pulled up, covers most of the face. In addition, he was wearing a knit cap which was pulled down low over his brow. Between the two pieces of clothing, it was impossible to see very much of his face. He did not look like a typical pecan picker.

I pay close attention when the hair on the back of my neck stands up. My pickup was the only vehicle in the driveway, so I believe that the visitor assumed I was alone. I explained that because of the liability and the fact that people who climb pecan trees tend to break branches, the answer was no. He walked away. I locked the door. I stood at the window for what I assumed was a reasonable amount of time and didn't see anything. I then went out to check on my pickup. The side by the street had been keyed, the window on that side had been smashed and a tire had been slashed.

As I stood there on the phone, the neighbor across the street came out and asked if I was calling the police. I said that I was.

He said, "Didn't you hear him smashing your window?"

I said, "I did not, nor did I see anything. Did you?"

"Yes."

"Did you call the police?"

"No. I went in the house."

That was the kind of neighborhood it was.

Of course they were never caught. I later took the truck to the auto body repair shop to have the damage repaired. This necessitated my renting a car for a week.

I left the car parked in my driveway for two days and then went to visit my cousin. I parked the car, and we only traveled in her car. This information is important because of what happened next.

I drove home and parked it for one more day. I then got a call from the car rental place and was told that I needed to bring the car in because it was going to an auction in El Paso and they needed it right away. I drove the car down to them. The manager said that he needed to inspect the returned car and have me sign a release before they would give me another car.

When he returned with the release form for me to sign, it said that there was damage to the car. I went with him to investigate. There was a nick the size of a pinhead on the exact edge of the driver's side door, which could not be seen when the door was closed. You cannot cheat an honest person because they strive to be very fair in all their dealings. I believe in this and live my life that way. I knew that I had not done the damage. The manager insisted that I had to sign the release form, so I wrote in large letters that I had not done any of the damage that was indicated on the form and signed it.

At the time I had a flip phone, so I had no way of taking a photograph. I called a friend to see if he would bring his camera. He told me that I should just pay for the damage because they could ruin my credit. I refused.

I subsequently received a bill in the amount of $246.00 (2009 dollars) from the rental company. That would be $353.00 in 2025 dollars. I called them and was told it was repaired and that was the amount of the damage.

I said, "I want to rent that car again, since you repaired it."

"We won't rent to you again because you have not paid for the damage you caused."

"Alright, I will pay for damage if you bring the car back to Roswell so I can take pictures of the repair."

"The car is not in town. I will send you a copy of the repair bill."

When I got the copy, it showed the amount and in the middle of the bill was a hand drawn smiley face.

I ignored the bill and then I started getting harassing phone calls with threats to turn me in to the credit bureau. I told them that it was a scam and to do what they needed to do.

They eventually quit calling and that was the end of that. I later read in a retirement magazine that a car rental company had been busted for doing this very thing to retirees. They didn't do it to this one!

Chapter 11
Latifa, Rowena and Bubba

The legal side of being a landlord: Get a copy of every police report. It gives you evidence and makes sure that your tenant follows through with prosecution. Let me tell you a story about this: I will call them Latifa, Bubba, and Bubba's ex-wife, Rowena. He cold cocked her. But wait! It started like this:

One time I checked on one of my rent houses and found a broken window. Latifa explained that Rowena had broken it because Bubba would not go outside to talk with her. Bubba had been living with Rowena prior to marrying Latifa. I told Latifa that if it happened again, she was to make a police report and that if she did not, I would evict her and Bubba.

I also told her to fix the window. Of course, they could not fix it because neither of them knew how to measure. When I found this out, I measured it for her, and they purchased and installed the glass. Not very expertly, but it kept out the wind.

Again, I went by and checked the house. I saw what appeared to be a pile of clothes under a tree, with a bicycle leaning up against the house. A closer inspection revealed that a skinny, baldheaded woman was sleeping soundly under the tree. I let the sleeping woman lie. I did, however, call the police and talk to the day commander.

I explained what the problem was and that I wanted to teach her a lesson by filing a criminal damage report. He laughed and said that he doubted that I could teach her anything because she had a rap sheet several pages long.

Another check of the house revealed another broken window. I knocked on the door and Latifa explained that Rowena had broken it again because Bubba wouldn't come out and talk to her.

I asked her if she filed a police report and she said, "No."

"I told you to file a report or I would evict you. Why didn't you do it?"

"Because Bubba knocked her out."

After hearing the entire story, I realized that we would have to wait until next time.

Rowena had tried to get Bubba's attention. She wanted him to come out and talk to her. He refused. She then hurled a rock through the window. Bubba came out of the house and cold cocked her. She lay there in the driveway until she regained consciousness. When she came to, she rode off on her bicycle.

Postscript to this story: Bubba finally moved out of Latifa's house and moved in with another woman. Thereafter, Rowena left Latifa alone.

SIGH.

Chapter 12
The Squatter

I was working for free for a property owner who lacked the ability to manage his rentals. I felt sorry for him because he seemed very timid. He was not able to deal with confrontations so when the tenants said they did not have the rent; he did not know what to do about it. I felt sorry for him because it looked like he was going to lose his properties. I was taking care of his fourplex and had cleaned up and rented each unit as I finished it.

There was one last efficiency apartment that I was repairing and cleaning. I noticed that there appeared to be someone using the apartment because I found cereal bowls in the sink and the oven was warm. There were also some blankets which were spread out behind the sofa. I threw them in the trash along with some clothes and personal items. I changed the lock on the door.

In a day or two I noticed that the lock had been jimmied. The items from the dumpster were again in the apartment. I called the owner, and he asked me to take care of it. I told him that this was a legal issue and since I was not his property manager he needed to be there when I called the police and made arrangements for a police visit. I called the police and asked them to show up at six o'clock AM the next day. They showed up, as did the owner. He introduced himself, said that I was acting on his behalf, and then went to hide out of sight.

The police knocked on the door. No answer. They tried the door. Locked. They said that no one was there and started to leave. I suggested that they announce themselves louder. They did. No answer. I asked them to break the door in since the lock had been jimmied and barely caught. They said they couldn't do that. I stepped forward and said that I would. I pushed the door with my shoulder, and it flew open.

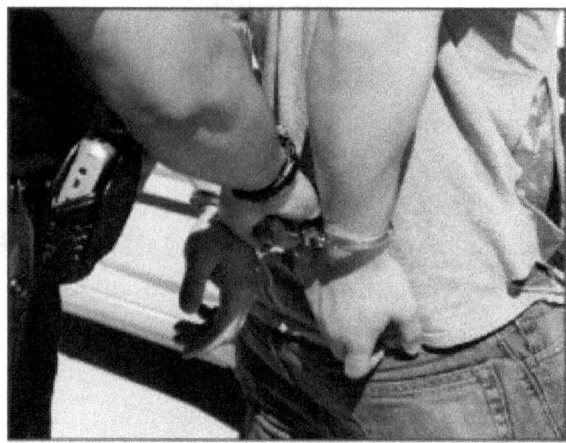

I charged in and immediately felt a tug on my shirt tail. I was pulled back out the door. One officer told me to step back, and they both went in. I followed. Gun drawn, the lead officer said, "Get out of there! Get out of there, NOW!" Soon a man emerged from the closet. The officers took him outside.

One officer asked him, "Why are you sweating?"

"I'm afraid."

"You should be. You are trespassing." The officer patted him down.

"What's that under your pants?"

"A colostomy bag."

The officer recoiled. I was asked what I wanted to do with him. I said that I would call the owner. He showed up a few minutes later and said that he wanted to turn the squatter loose if he promised to never show up there again.

The officer asked, "Do you promise never to show up here again?" The squatter nodded. He was let go. I cleaned the apartment.

Chapter 13
Tracking the Bull

I needed to buy another bull. Because I worked full time I had very limited time to shop. The local sale barn is not always the best place to buy livestock because frequently, when ranchers have a problem animal, they will run it through a sale barn. What you see is what you get. As is. No refunds. I took the day off from work, so I could look over what was available that week. I bought a good-looking black Angus bull with the brand of a ranch which had a reputation for producing good calves. That was about the best I could do.

I paid for him and had the cowboys at the pens brand him for me. They have the personnel and equipment to handle that sort of thing easily. I drove through to the loading pen. When the guys tried to load that big, black, beautiful bull, he was pretty fractious so they would not get behind him. They were waiting for him to load by himself. I said that I would run him into the trailer if they promised to shut the middle gate as soon as I got him into the front section.

They did indeed slam the gate, but they slammed it so hard that it bounced and started to come open. I was barely fast enough to slam the gate and get it to catch before that bull swapped ends and was looking at me, eyeball to eyeball, about two feet away. From my peripheral vision I saw an arm reach up and hold the latch on the gate. I scrambled out of the trailer and locked the back gate.

I took him down to the pasture to drop him off with the cows. I knew that three cows were in heat. He never even looked at them. He headed south, jumped the fence and was gone. This started a two-week odyssey. I worked all day, six days a week, so I had little time to chase cows.

On my first day off, I looked for him and saw tracks. I asked the man who owned the land that I leased to help me because the bull was a master of evasion. The next week, I walked and Pigner drove the pickup. I tracked the bull across two pastures, probably four miles. I could tell as the tracks got fresher that we were closing in. I tracked him back and forth across the river and through stands of salt cedar trees and cane.

When I finally found him, it was unexpected. He was standing very still, and I was about twenty feet from him. I don't know how long he had been watching me. Apparently, he did not think I was a threat since I was afoot. I waved to Pigner, and he drove closer to me. The bull broke for the river. I started running as fast as I could to cut him off from the river. I thought I was headed for a clump of dried tumbleweeds and was prepared to charge through it. I tumbled ass over tea kettle into a ditch. Ouch!! That hurt!

I got behind the bull and started driving him back to my pasture. A horse would not have helped at this point. He would not leave the trees, so I had to climb over logs and push aside large weeds to drive him in the direction of my pasture. At one point he got close to the water and stood in the cane. I walked past him and would have lost him if I had not heard him pee. I circled back and got behind him, crowding him along.

At this point we had been playing hide and seek for a few hours in the salt cedars. He got hot and lay down in the shadows, watching me. When I got too close, he stood up and started towards me. I ducked behind the largest, nearest tree and stood still until he turned and started back the way I was trailing him. I stayed on his tail, so he tried another tactic. He ran out of the trees about 300 feet and quickly lay down in the tall grass and weeds in the pasture.

I could not see him, so Pigner stood on top of the truck to spot him. When he found him, he drove him homewards. I stayed close to the trees so he would not get back to the river's edge. We got him to the gate between the pastures which we had left open. YES! We were almost home. We saw the bull look at the ground in front of him and bolt for the river. When we got up to the gate we saw an empty package of chicken gizzards. Damn fishermen! We had been at this all day!

Pigner called in a day or two and said that a neighbor had gathered his cattle, and my bull was among them.

"What do you want me to do with him?"

"Take him to the sale barn!"

Pigner called me a few weeks later and told me that the bull had gone through a sale barn further north. That was smart of whoever owned him at the time. By this time, he had at least three brands on him. He was getting a bad reputation around my neck of the woods.

Chapter 14
The Story of Daft

This is a story about a screwball that I rented to when I was managing some houses for a landlord—For Free. The owner was about to lose everything because he could not deal with the tenants. The fact that he was a heavy marijuana user might have had something to do with it. I did not know this at the time.

Anyway, I will call the tenant Daft for reasons that will become abundantly clear. I first met her when she called about a two-bedroom house that I was managing, for free. She was staying in a room at a flea-bitten motel which had been provided to her by the police department. I took her to the house. She liked it and we made a rental arrangement. She and her two dogs moved in.

Daft bought a car. The car did not run very reliably. She also could not register it because she did not have the title for the car. One day she got a ticket, which required that she go to Municipal Court. Her car would not start. She visited a neighbor and asked for a ride to court. The neighbor refused. When Daft left their yard, she took their weed eater.

The neighbor called the police and Daft was arrested. She was put in a psychiatric facility for evaluation. I learned about this when I found an unknown woman in her house, going through her things. She said that Daft had asked her to get her glasses and meds because she was in jail. The woman explained to me that my offer to visit her would be rejected because unless an inmate lists a person as a visitor, they are not allowed to visit. She had not listed me as a permitted visitor so I could not see her. I'm sure that if she had been in her right mind, she would have wanted me to visit, if for no other reason than to try to get her out of jail.

I talked to her attorney and offered to help in any way that I could. When her trial date came up, I attended the court hearing. The judge was not going to let her out until her attorney told the judge that I agreed to be responsible for her. She was not a danger to herself or others, she simply had trouble functioning. She was released based on my keeping an eye on her. She told me that she was moving to Texas, and I lost track of her.

Many months later I saw her at a shopping mall. She was trying to get a ride somewhere. She was in a wheelchair. I found out that she was homeless, and the police had picked her up again. They gave her a couple of days free at a local motel, again.

I told her that I had a house I was working on and that if she wanted to stay there, she was welcome. I put her in the house and gave her boxes of food, bedding, dog food and other things.

When she received her government check, she went across the street and talked those people into renting her a room. Ka-ching. They saw free money. I asked for my key back and she complied. When I went to work on the house several days later, I found it odd that the blinds were open when I had closed them, and I spotted cigarette ashes by the window. I changed the locks.

The neighbor came by and told me the rest of the story. Daft moved in and was not a good tenant. She soon started asking for a return of the rent so she could buy cigarettes and things. She was argumentative and disruptive. She could certainly be that way if she did not get what she wanted!

Within the month they kicked her out of the house. She started spending the night in my house, using a copy of the key she had returned to me. This was one time when I did not change the lock. I should have!

Daft came by one day and wanted me to help her find a home. I made an effort to get her located but she did not like the places that I found for her. I'm sure that she was expecting me to put her in one of my houses. She had burned that bridge. I heard stories of her bothering people, but I never saw her again. You just can't help some people.

Chapter 15
Accused of Kidnapping

I was once accused, from the witness stand, of kidnapping a tenant. She swore under oath that it was true. Here is the real story.

I was visiting with a neighbor when her cleaning lady showed up. I will refer to her as Troublemaker. She was crying and had bruises up and down her arms. She said that her alcoholic boyfriend kept telling her to get out of the house they shared and yet he demanded that she give him her paycheck.

We asked her if she wanted to leave him, and she said yes. I offered to put her and her son in a vacant house I owned if she promised that she would not tell her boyfriend where she went. She promised and assured us that she wanted to get away from him. We then made a plan for the following day. The neighbor and I would each take a flatbed trailer with our pickups, and I would also bring one young man, whom I paid, to help load the furniture. She said that her son would also help.

The boyfriend showed up while we were there and threatened Troublemaker, shoving her into a corner and choking her. I immediately announced that I was calling the Police Department and Boyfriend lunged at me in a threatening manner. I stared him down and said, "Go ahead. I have the Police on the line." When the Police showed up, Boyfriend was arrested for domestic violence. We continued packing and got her moved. One thing we found was a three-foot lead pipe, filled with something heavy, hidden behind a chair. We took that too.

In a couple of weeks, the neighbor and I sat outside the courtroom with the arresting officer, while the hearing took place. The officer had quit his job and was a police officer in a nice ski community in the northern part of the state. He took the day off to drive across the state and testify at this trial.

I was called into the courtroom and sworn in. The attorney for the defendant tried to rattle me by accusing me of things. He said that I was a tax evader because I was paying people under the table. I told him that my CPA told me that if I did not pay anyone more than six hundred dollars in a year that I did not have to declare it.

The attorney then said that Troublemaker had said under oath that the neighbor and I had kidnapped her, against her will, and forced her to move into my house. I said that we had better things to do and asked him why I would have done that. His reply surprised me.

He said it was because I was having an affair with the Troublemaker's son and that was why I moved them into one of my houses. The son was about twenty years old at the time, and I was nearly seventy. I answered that there were three of us, each of us being around seventy years old and that our interest was only to provide help for Troublemaker and her son.

Her son had been born and raised on a Reservation, and we were trying to change the trajectory of his life. We had gone in together to hire an attorney for the son. Son had gotten drunk and stole and wrecked a car. Two friends and I had joined together to help him out of his trouble. We were in court when the sentence was passed and he got a light sentence because his attorney drew the judge's attention to us, sitting in a back row, and said that we were there to help the boy change. The two other women felt he was worth saving. I had some reservations but went along with the whole thing. This brings to mind the saying, "In for a dollar, in for a dime."

The attorney then asked why we were trying so hard to help the son when he was a troublemaker. I looked straight at the boyfriend and said, "Because he has never had a father figure in his life." The attorney then dismissed me, and I had to leave the courtroom. My neighbor was then called in to testify. He accused her of the same things.

The jails in the area were full at the time and prisoners were being sent to jails in Texas. That might be why the boyfriend got off with probation. There is a lot of domestic violence in this town so maybe choking someone is not a serious enough problem to warrant jail time. I don't know. Troublemaker moved out of my house and moved back in with her boyfriend. Her son went to jail for the auto theft.

When he got out of jail, I bought a small trailer for him to live in, for free, and bought him several hundred dollars' worth of food and clothes. I then got him in touch with his eight-year-old daughter whom he had not seen in years.

The three of us old women paid for him to start college and got him a job with a roofer. He started drinking and using drugs. I had to evict him from the trailer. His life went downhill. But that is another story. You just can't help some people.

Chapter 16
Sue-Happy Sara

Sue-Happy Sara learned about unintended consequences the hard way. I posted a Three-Day Notice of Failure to Pay Rent on her door. It stated that she now owed the rent plus a late fee. She was late with the rent and apparently thought that she could intimidate me by sending me a certified letter with demands for alterations to the house, citing her children's illnesses as the basis for these demands. This action does not relieve a tenant from paying the rent, but a lot of people do not know that. This attempt at legal intimidation apparently had worked for her in the past.

The letter included a demand that I recarpet the house, install new weather stripping on all the windows, replace the screen door, repair the bathroom sink and toilet, and fix the leak in the backyard "which smells like sewer."

By way of explanation let me say that I never rent a house until I have made it ready to move in because I don't want to work in a house with someone living there. Sue-Happy Sara had only been in the house for a few months.

An inspection of the house revealed that someone had flushed a toy down the toilet (blocking the bathroom drains), the screen door needed a screw tightened, and the water in the backyard was the result of someone using a post-hole digger while building a dog run, thus chipping the water line. The evidence of this was a pair of post hole diggers leaning against the house.

I fired back a certified letter telling her when and how I would fix the things that I needed to fix and offering to let her out of the item of the contract which required a thirty-day notice before vacating the rental. I also expressed concern for the health of her children and suggested that they find a house that suited them as quickly as possible.

I soon received an invective-laced phone call from the grandmother. I tried to explain to the grandmother of the supposedly sick children that since my house was being blamed for the multiple illnesses of the children, I did not want to hinder them in any way from seeking a healthier environment. I suggested that they move at their earliest convenience. She continued ranting and threatening until I hung up. The woman either did not understand the content of my letter or was being deliberately obtuse. Sometimes it is hard to tell the difference. I suspect that her anger was the result of the family not getting the desired result from their demand letter.

I filed a Three-Day Notice for Nonpayment of Rent and in ten days we were in court. You should know that in New Mexico, at least, only the Judge can "evict" a tenant. Don't ever state, in front of a Judge, that you have posted an eviction notice. They take umbrage at that. I made that mistake just once and was told, "Nobody evicts but me!"

The Magistrate judge ruled in my favor, sort of, and she was ordered to pay court costs in the amount of one hundred and two dollars. She was not required to pay the past due rent or the late fee. She had already moved out.

A postscript to this story is in order here. Sue-Happy Sara then paid one hundred and seventeen dollars to file in District Court, appealing the verdict of the lower court, which was in the amount of one hundred and two dollars. This was a Court fee, not my late fee. As I write this, I can't remember her ever paying the court-ordered settlement.

I called my attorney, because a person should have one in District Court due to the procedures being more formal. A person must give a formal, written answer to all pleas. After listening to my presentation of the facts, he said, "You don't have to worry. You have done as good a job as I could with the presentation and the judge is going to be fuming under his robes when he hears this case."

She told her story in court and waved a stack of medical bills, claiming that they were the result of living in my house for several months. I pointed out that she had six dogs, and she was allowed to have two. I had photographs to support my claim. The judge remarked that it could possibly be the six dogs running in and out of the house that had caused her children's allergies.

After the District Court Judge heard all the evidence on both sides, he upheld the Lower Court verdict. It cost me an attorney consultation to be vindicated. I don't know what possessed her to tell the judge the following, as part of her argument.

She told the District Court Judge that she had mental problems. Was this an insanity plea? I don't know. I also don't know which planet she came from. Maybe the undiscovered planet of Bat Crap Crazy. It seems to have a lot of inhabitants.

As it turned out, I got a call from the Welfare Fraud Department and I was able to give them useful information that the tenant revealed in court, under oath, which supported a case of welfare fraud against her.

It still cost me to go to the District Court. That is what attorneys are for. I just wrote it off my income tax and tried to forget about it. It's the time and wear and tear on my nerves that I couldn't write off. I never heard from her again. When I remember this, I shake my head, at me and her.

Chapter 17
The Bicyclist

One night I was called to one of the houses that I managed and found a man in the tool shed. I'll call him Biker. I called the police, but they were too busy to come since it was not a residential invasion, so I accosted the man myself.

He said that he was helping my tenant and that he was living in the tent in her backyard. I called her to verify this. She explained that he sometimes helped her, so she let him live in her backyard. Well, technically it was my backyard, but she rented it along with the house. That seemed to be a gray area in our rental agreement, so I let it pass. I could have used the clause in the contract that states that an extra person will require an additional $100 per month, but I did not.

Sometime later she moved to another of my houses. I then found out that Biker was sleeping in the doorway of a nearby school. There had been reports of a mountain lion around the area. I told the man that if he wanted to live in one of my empty houses, I would furnish the house, utilities, a refrigerator, and microwave for free. I told him I would give him five dollars an hour if he worked two or three mornings a week for me.

He moved in and immediately got sick. Biker was eating food out of the dumpsters. I bought him medicine and brought him food for about seven days before he could work. I helped him get on food stamps. He did not have any ID and since he did not have an address, he could not get the stamps. I got all of that taken care of for him. He would not go to the food pantry or YMCA because he did not want to sit through the 30-minute sermon at either place that provided food. He had a buggy attached to his bicycle. He would go to the convenience stores, Pizza Hut and KFC at closing times and negotiate for free food.

I gave him the address of one of my houses and told him to paint the cabinets white. I left a gallon of white paint on the counter. When I went by one night to see what he had done, he had painted the cabinets green. In my discussion with him, it became evident that he had found some paint and expected me to pay him for the use of it. I did not. I also told him that I would not pay him for the work he had done.

I then asked to be introduced to the girl who was sitting in the living room, smoking pot. He introduced me. I asked him to meet me at another house in the morning because a sewer was stopped up and I was going to rent a machine and rod it out. He did not show up.

I went to get the router and did the cleanout with the help of the tenant. NEVER do this alone. You can lose a finger. One plumber that I knew of was working alone with a router and was electrocuted. Never, ever do it alone! It is worth it to call a professional. But I digress.

After we unclogged the line and loaded up the equipment, I headed back to the rental place and who should cross my path but Biker!? The girl was sitting cross-legged in the buggy. He waved and continued on his merry way.

It wasn't long before he started hiding from me. I went into a hardware store one day and they asked about him. I said that I couldn't find him. I was told that he had been hiding in there. He had told them that I would not pay him to work. They were quite surprised to find out that I was not only paying him, but I was furnishing him a house, utilities, appliances, et cetera, for free.

One time I went to the house to pick him up. I knocked on the front door and called his name. I went around to the back of the house in time to see his feet disappearing through the bedroom window. When I stuck my head in the window to ask what he was doing, he told me that he was sick.

The next incident occurred soon after this. I went by the house and the front door was open. Inside I could see Biker and another man working on bicycles. The built-in shelves were filled with little trinkets and things that he must have scavenged from dumpsters, such as picture frames, figurines and bottles. The way they were all arranged, it looked like he might have been preparing to open a second-hand store.

I told Biker why I was canceling our agreement. I took their pictures up close and told them to get out of my house. I also told them that if I saw them around my house or if there was any damage, I would call the police. And that was that!

Chapter 18
Southern Engineering

This story goes back to a time when I still had my two girls at home. I also had three foster girls. Two were teens and one was about 10. I had purchased a 1958 Chrysler Saratoga for my oldest daughter. Because the mother of the three girls refused to sign a release so that they could ride the bus to school, it fell on me, as their foster mother, to provide transportation to and from school and any activities they were engaged in.

The girls loved that big, roomy car. It drew a lot of attention since it was some twenty odd years old by the time my daughter owned it. It looked like the Batmobile. That is what they called it.

I went to the local gas station and told the owner that I was going to send my daughter in to get new tires and wanted him to order whatever was required for the car. When he called and said that the tires were in, I sent my daughter with a check to pay for the tires and get them installed. This comes into play later in this story.

I worked six days a week in a town about 25 miles away from home. On this particular Saturday, I was tasked with putting an inter-liner in two pairs of very tall drapes. The customer insisted that her windows not be left uncovered overnight. I took them down and was busy in the shop taking them apart when I got a phone call from my oldest daughter. They had come to town and were stuck.

The car had sprung a leak, and they had parked it beside a Chinese restaurant. It was summertime. The heat was oppressive. I went to where they were waiting in the heat, beside the car, and loaded them all in my pickup. I took them to the public library and told them I would pick them up as soon as I finished working on and rehanging the draperies.

It was after six when I finished and picked up the girls. I drove to the Chinese restaurant and lay down as far under the car as I could go. I determined that a radiator hose had sprung a leak. This presented a problem. The two auto supply stores were already closed.

There was no Walmart, Target, or K-Mart in town. I went to a grocery store and bought several gallons of water and a large roll of duct tape and a roll of electric tape. I figured that the electric tape could be stretched tightly around the hose but might not hold when the hot water started flowing. So, since duct tape was meant to tape heating ducts, it should all hold long enough to get my family safely home. This was southern engineering at its best.

I returned to the car, lifted the hood so I had as much light as possible, lay on the hot pavement and scooted as far under the car as possible. This was difficult since the man who sold me the tires had put the wrong size on the car. It sat low to the ground. My daughter did not inform me of that fact. As I lay there tightly wrapping the tape around the radiator hose, a shadow fell across my work. I looked up to see an old Chinese gentleman with a very wrinkled face peering down at me.

"May I help you?" I asked.

"No." He responded.

He continued to stare at me, so I continued with the task at hand.

When I felt that I had temporarily fixed the problem, I slid out from under the car and stood up. The gentleman straightened and looked up at me.

"You one very smart lady."

"Thank you." I replied.

Postscript: I got the girls home safely. On Monday I bought a new radiator hose.

Chapter 19
The Day of the Air Show

There was the time I oversaw the VIP tents for an Air Show. This involved getting the volunteers, coordinating with the caterers, setting up the interiors of the tents and coordinating things with other managers for time and insurance. That is an interesting thing. You don't just buy a policy for an event. I don't remember exactly how it worked but you had to buy for a specific period of time. The shorter the time, the less it cost. We all met for organization. First monthly, then weekly, then daily as we got to within a week of the opening date. On the opening day the walkie talkies were full of constant chatter. This enabled us to solve any problems quickly.

Managing the volunteers takes a special skill. Since they are not getting paid you must find out their motive for volunteering and try to play to that. Some want to have a front row seat to the Air Show itself and be out of the sun. All the public, except those under the tents, are on the Tarmac, which gets pretty warm in the summer. Some are hungry for socializing, some perceive it as a prestigious endeavor, some are there for the free food and beer and some just want to be a part of something. They are subject to quitting on you if you don't address whatever their reason is for being there, or if their feelings get hurt.

Buying a tent entitles the purchaser to host a certain number of people. Usually, twenty or so. The volunteers make sure that everyone is served and is comfortable and that their tent area stays clean. Some of the tent renters allow the volunteers to interact with the guests and others want them to keep their mouths shut and act like waiters and waitresses. That was back in a time before servers came to a restaurant table and gave you their name and tried to interact with you.

Matching the volunteer to the personality of the host of each of these tents required a type of diplomacy which was not something in which I was very experienced. My attitude has always been that if something needs to be done then just do it.

I had to make sure that the tubs of beer under the tables were far enough inside that kids couldn't reach under the tents and snag the alcohol. This was a constant problem.

Before the gates opened, I was able to visit some of the displays. The Air Force brought in some of the aircraft including the F15. I went to see it and there were men facing me with some heavy-duty weapons. They did not smile. I did not get as close as I wanted to. They were serious. I moved on. I looked through other planes including the Columbine II which was the first Air Force I which President Eisenhower rode in. I then studied a large cargo plane and asked the guard many questions about how far it could fly before refueling, etc. Then I asked him how many tanks would fit in the cargo bay. I don't know if he was being smart or was tired of answering questions.

Anyway, he said, "If I tell you, I will have to kill you."

I immediately replied, "Is it worth dying for?" He tried to keep the smile off his face as I moved on. So—Back to work. I checked each tent and the volunteers, giving them words of encouragement and the gates were opened. People began filling the tents and I changed some of the volunteers around to make everybody happy.

We kept getting updates on the weather. The wind was picking up. I had been outvoted about the table decorations. There were paper decorations on the serving tables surrounding the small open fire burners which were keeping the food warm. After two table fires, I took down all the decorations. The wind was getting more intense. Soon there was an announcement that some of the smaller planes and acrobatic acts were canceling. The insurance was locked into a short time frame. The longer the time frame, the more money the insurance cost.

Soon there was trash blowing and then the tents started rippling. I knew I was on my own getting about two hundred people out of the confined area in a calm and organized manner. I started at one end and evacuated the tents, explaining that the event was canceled, there would be an announcement about reimbursement and please exit to your vehicles as quickly as possible. Because there were so many elderly people it was time-consuming trying to get everyone moving towards the parking lot without causing undue worry. I made sure that each tent was empty and turned off the propane burners and ushered everyone out of each tent before I went to the next one. Some of the volunteers had abandoned their post and many people were scared, confused and waiting for directions.

I looked back and saw the tents collapsing and some were rising into the air. By the time I got to the last tent I found one young woman who told me that she was going to sue us because she had hurt her head on a table. I knew her and talked firmly to her, explaining that if she tried to take advantage of the situation, it would not go well for her. I knew that she was looking for a job and explained that a lot of very important people were on the board of the Air Show, and she would be blacklisted for trying to fake an injury. She got up and left.

By now the tent poles were dancing. Because the young woman was seated and in discussion with me, people were not moving. By the time I got her up and out, I had to hold on to one of the front tent poles which was jumping about two feet off the ground. When I looked up, I saw one of the board members holding onto the opposite pole. As soon as the last person vacated the tent he said, "Are we ready?" I said, "yes." and we let go of the poles and jumped back to prevent being smacked by them as the tent was airborne.

I then went back through the area seeing what needed to be done, including moving people out of the larger area of the tarmac. By now there were police cars, and I was able to put some of the most infirm in the cars.

We were called to a meeting in a hangar. As the one in charge of the tents I was asked how I wanted to handle it. I said that the trauma was a lot for everybody so I would like to wait until tomorrow and I would call some groups to help with clean up. The next day we gave free entry to anyone who wanted to come out for the show. It was a pretty small crowd. The reason that there had been such a large crowd the day before was because a very famous country singer was performing.

I was wearing cowboy boots, jeans, an Air Show T-shirt and a narrow-brimmed cowboy hat. White straw with a teal-colored hat band decorated with beads and ribbons. I referred to it as my rich-b—-ch hat. That getup made me about six feet tall. Someone followed me around taking pictures. I don't know who it was. I don't have any pictures of that nerve-wracking day. I just know that at the end of the day, I sure could have used a hug and a drink. Not necessarily in that order. And I never did get my promised ride in a helicopter.

Chapter 20
Lulu the Laundress

As is my custom, I did a landlord drive by on one of my rentals. I found what appeared to be a blazing campfire under a tree in the front yard. The lights were off in the house, the front door was open, and a fly catcher was taped to the door frame. Several guests were gathered around the fire. They did not appear to be roasting hot dogs or toasting marshmallows. This caused me great concern because of the proximity of the fire to the tree, and the proximity of the tree to the house. I called the Fire Department to check on the legality of this activity.

I was told that as long as the fire was "not too large" I had no cause for a complaint.

Sooooo....... Another drive by and I noticed that there were several five-gallon buckets sitting around the yard. Not under the tree and not surrounding the fire. Studying the scene more closely, I noticed that the buckets were right side up. This is not a very comfortable position if the buckets are intended to be used as seating. I called the tenant's brother. I will call him Edwardo. When I asked Edwardo why there were so many buckets in the front yard, he explained that they were doing their laundry. I then asked why they did not use their washing machine. He said he did not know and suggested that maybe it was broken. I am a little slow to catch on sometimes, but I finally did. I called the Electric Company, and they said that they had shut off the power to the house.

I then called the Water Company and was told that the water had been turned off. I did another drive by and noticed that a hose was draped over the fence between the neighbor's house and theirs. They apparently were using the neighbor's water (which is illegal.) What a sleuth I am! I immediately called Edwardo and set up a meeting with him.

I told him that I would post a Thirty Day Notice instead of a Seven Day Notice if he would promise to have his father and sister removed in that period of time. I could have posted a Seven Day Notice but since they were on government assistance and only received one check a month; it would have been useless to try to move them out any sooner.

Also, it takes at least 10 days to get on the court docket and the judge will usually give them seven days to move. See how the math works? When you run up against these types of things, always pause to think about the legal ramifications. Sometimes discretion is the wisest action.

Postscript to the story is this: The inspector in charge of fraud for the Power Company called me to investigate "the improper use of the electrical equipment." He informed me that the power had been turned off at the pole.

Apparently, Lulu the Laundress and Luis the Liar (her father), had removed the glass case from the meter and somehow jumped a wire so that the power was on but did not read on the meter. My heart jumped because the law reads that if the power is turned off at the main power pole, which the Power Company had done, I could be required to do a complete upgrade of the electrical system. This could have cost me several thousand dollars.

I explained the situation I had with the tenants and that I had given them a Thirty Day Notice. The investigator expressed appreciation for my cooperation and hung up. I talked to Edwardo. He promised to have them out of the house by the fifth of the following month. We shook hands and I told him that I depended on his word as a gentleman. It turned out that they had used another person's identity to turn on the electrical service.

I received another call from the fraud department of the Power Company. The person whose identity they used to turn on the power was filing a charge against Lulu. I again explained what I was doing to remove them from my house.

When I got them out and called to have the power turned back on there was not a problem and no call for an upgrade to the electrical system. Thank You! Thank You!

Chapter 21
Agnes

I had one bizarre incident that happened several years ago. Agnes applied to rent one of the houses. She had two teenage boys and one boy about age 10. When her boyfriend unloaded her things, he unloaded a stove. Since I furnished the stove and refrigerator, she asked if I would store hers.

I agreed. The children started school and everything seemed all right. Then she called to tell me that they had no hot water. I went to check on it and found that the TP valve on the hot water heater was open in overflow mode, running constantly, and had flooded the living room carpet. I suspected that one of the boys had fooled around with it. That did not matter, I still had to fix it and dry out the carpet.

Since one of the teens was lying on the floor watching television, I asked why I had not been informed of this before it became such a problem. The child- looked up at me and said, "Oh yeah, Mom told me to call you."

I asked where his mother was and was told that she was out of town. The next month I could not get hold of her to collect the rent. After several trips to the house, it became obvious that she was dodging me.

I finally posted a Three-Day Notice of Non-Payment of Rent Notice. Remember that landlords do not evict. Only the judge can evict! I then got a call from Agnes, stating that she was moving and wanted her stove. I told her that as soon as she paid the past due rent and I did an inspection, I would turn the stove over to her.

I next heard from an appliance company in another town. They told me that she had not made payments, and they wanted their stove back. I told them the story and told the caller that I could not turn over a tenant's property to anyone but the tenant. They warned me of the consequences if I did not comply with their request. Threats have never been very effective on me. I explained my position again.

The next phone call was from a television news reporter. I wonder who called them. Nosy Nelly said that she had gotten a phone call about a slumlord situation and that she had gone to investigate. Nosy Nelly said that the ceiling was falling down in the bathroom. Upon inspection it turned out that they had hooked the water hose to the evaporative cooler and left the water running. Had they called me, I would have adjusted the float. Simple fix. Instead, the knuckleheads had left the water running and the evaporative cooler overflowed into the house, caving in the ceiling.

The reporter said that the house was filthy and there appeared to be several teenagers and a disabled ten-year-old living there without supervision. I said that I would call the police about that.

Nosy Nelly, sensing a story about slumlords, asked for an interview for the evening news and threatened to put this mess on the air and make me look bad if I did not comply. I explained the situation to the best of my knowledge. I told Nosy Nelly that I would give her the names of my other tenants as character witnesses but that if they or I ended up on the news, I would file a lawsuit.

I explained that I did take very good care of my tenants and the houses. When she realized that I couldn't be bullied, she volunteered that there appeared to be something wrong with the scene when she went to investigate because there were several teenagers and the disabled boy and no evidence of any adult presence. And yet she was willing to drag my name through the mud for a news story!

When I finally got them all out and went to clean the house, a neighbor volunteered the rest of the story.

Apparently, the mother had a new boyfriend who did not want the children, so she brought them to a town ninety miles from where she lived and rented my house for them. The postscript to this story is that two weeks later, there was a two-part expose about bad tenants and bad landlords. My name was not mentioned.

Chapter 22
Betty and Rodger

I met Betty and Rodger when I joined a Bible study group. They were retired and on a small income. Whenever I was close to them, I noticed the faint whiff of sewer gas. They did not seem to know that they smelled. One thing about smells like that is that when you live in a house with smells you become inured to it.

As I got to know them, and they found out that I had rentals, they broached the subject of the sewer line problems that they were having. They said that they had two bathrooms and whenever they had guests, the second bath always backed up in the shower and the toilet would not flush.

I asked if they had routed out the line. Yes, they had. I offered to go and look at it, but they declined. I didn't know why, but I respected their decision. They still seemed to want my advice if not my help. I then suggested that they use the router down the vent pipe. Rodger did that. It did not work.

They finally accepted my offer to look at the problem when I gently told them that their clothes smelled of sewer gas. They were terribly embarrassed and asked me why I didn't tell them before. I explained that since they couldn't do anything about it, I did not want to embarrass them.

I went to their house and checked things out. There is only so much you can see without cameras. I suggested that Rodger cut a hole in the floor of the closet in the second bedroom so we could see under the house. That would be under the carpet and not show when repaired.

Here is what I found: 1. The house had a concrete pier running down the center of the house so no one could get through the hole and get to the plumbing. 2. There was an old cast iron or clay sewer pipe. (At this point, I can't remember which.) It was shaped in a Y. Only one connection was made to the new sewer line. The other side of the Y had been capped. Rodger, however, had punched the cap off the casing when he routed the line. This was the source of the sewer gas.

I took the man who helped me with my rentals to the house. I knew that they couldn't pay him so I said that if Rodger would help me fix an evaporative cooler, I would pay my helper, Alejandro. My cooler repair took an hour, his plumbing took all day. Fair enough.

I had Alejandro cut a hole in the floor in front of the toilet large enough for him to get under the house. The knuckleheads who plumbed the house put the sweeps upside down so that debris from the master bathroom washed into the sweep in the guest bathroom. It stayed there until someone used the guest bath, and the debris washed back into the other line. I went to the store and bought the parts needed and directed Alejandro into how to install them correctly.

The next problem was harder to solve. Rodger and I went around town trying to find the proper size cap for the open side of the Y. No such thing existed. The cap had been set loosely on the pipe and caulked. When Rodger used the router, he punched the cap off the line. That is why the house and people smelled of sewer gas. I then came up with a solution. I could not find any oakum. That is an old-time caulking used by many repair people. We went to a tire store and got a used inner tube. I cut two circles larger than the drain and instructed Alejandro to put caulk on top of the pipe, put the circles on top of the pipe and gently tap the cap down over the pipe. He then caulked the bottom edge of the cap.

I then showed him how to repair the floor. He caulked the seams, and a small rug covered our tracks. Everything worked fine and the odor cleared up. A few months later I got a call from Betty. She said that Rodger had cut a hole in the bathroom floor and could not repair it. I went to their house and found that he had taken a circular saw and butchered the floor. I asked Betty why he did that. She said that Rodger was slipping into dementia and his health was failing. He told her that he wanted to check on the plumbing to make sure that everything was OK before he died.

I went to the local store and tried to find matching wood laminate. There was a sample of what I needed but no boxes of flooring. I asked the department head when he would be getting more in. He said that they would not. I asked for the sample. He said no. I then explained the situation and reasoned with him. If he was not going to get in any more for a while, he would not need the sample, and my elderly couple NEEDED to repair their bathroom floor for safety reasons. He relented and gave me the sample. It was large enough. I then patched the floor, for a second time, and made Rodger promise not to touch it again. He died a few weeks later, secure in the knowledge that the plumbing was fixed.

Chapter 23
The Hole that Didn't Eat the House

One Christmas Eve day I got a call from one of my tenants. He was renting a small two-bedroom house. He was alarmed and called with an urgent voice wanting my immediate attention. He said that there was a huge hole in the back yard, and he was afraid that it was going to swallow the house. I assured him that considering the location of the house in the city, it was highly unlikely that the house would disappear into a hole. No, I did not know what it was and would come immediately.

When I got to the rent house, John excitedly met me in front of the house and led me to the back yard. It was indeed a large hole, about six feet by six feet and eight feet deep. He was visibly upset and kept expressing his concern about the house falling in. I explained that it was an old cesspool which had been abandoned when the sewer line was connected to the city sewer line many years ago.

He asked, "How do you know that?" I replied, "Well, first, I obviously did not know this when I bought the house. I have owned it for several years and there was no indication of a sink hole. I can tell what it is for several reasons. First is the proximity to the house. Second is the fact that the hole is square and obviously hand dug. The edges are straight. There is some rotten wood debris in the bottom which was apparently put on top of the hole before it was covered with dirt."

It had been mowed over without causing any problems for a long time. Since the city only gets about thirteen inches a year and most rains are less than one inch at a time, the ground dries up quickly, which is why the wooden covering lasted so long. I continued, "John, this is not a big problem, I can get it filled in after the holidays. Keep your family out of the back yard. Don't let the kids play around it." I put up stakes and caution tape around the hole, again assuring him that this was not a big problem.

After Christmas, I called a sand and gravel operation and talked to the owner, Darryl. I explained what I needed. He said that he would come out, when he had time, to assess the situation. I told him that I wanted to be there. He agreed. In January he called to give me an estimate and I agreed to the cost. I mentioned that he had not called me before going to the property and that I wanted to be there when the dirt was delivered. John called in a few days to say that the dirt was in front of the house. I went to check on the delivery.

The large pile of dirt was dumped in the only place in the front yard which blocked access to the hole in the back yard. It could have been dumped on the street at the curb, or in the gravel driveway or across the street in an empty lot. Instead, it was dumped on the small front lawn, blocking the approximately nine-foot access between the chain link side fence and the house.

I again called the contractor and told him that he had not notified me when the dirt was going to be delivered, and I wanted to be contacted before the tractor showed up to fill the hole and I told him that the dirt was blocking the only access to the backyard. Once again, I was not called.

In a few days I went by the house and found this mess. 1. The chain link fence in the front yard had been damaged. It separated my property from the neighbors. Apparently, the tractor hung up on the fence and stretched it out of shape. 2. A large branch from the tree in the front yard was broken off. 3. The sidewalk from the porch to the street was broken in several places where the tractor had run over it, and 4. The eave of the house was damaged. To say that I was angry would be a serious understatement.

I wrote Darryl a letter, on my letterhead, enumerating all the stupid mistakes which had been made and saying that had he discussed things with me all of this could have been avoided. I wanted to wet down the dirt as it was being put in the hole so it would pack down and not leave a sink hole. I demanded another load of dirt be delivered.

In a couple of days, Darryl left a phone message stating that the dirt had been delivered, for free, and he hoped that satisfied me! His voice was tight with anger. Did I care? He was not even man enough to talk to me on the phone, much less in person. I was mad enough to punch him. I did not want him sending any more idiots out to "fix" things, so I did not pursue any further action.

I dug up and re-poured the sidewalk, repaired the fence, cut the tree limb so it would heal, repaired the eave of the house and slowly filled in the hole by moving one wheelbarrow of dirt at a time and alternately soaking the dirt so it would settle. I then reseeded the area and asked John to keep it watered.

Taking Darryl to court would have taken time and money, in case you wonder. If you have read my book The Rental Roller Coaster, you already know how useless that would be.

All these problems could have been avoided if Darryl had not been so averse to meeting with "a woman" who knew what needed to be done. I had been told in the past that "we don't need any women on this job." By different men on different job sites. Sometimes it wasn't the words so much as the attitude. I had to deal with a lot of Darryls while I ranched and had rentals. It never got any easier. Women now don't know how much easier it is to get things done.

Chapter 24
The Tornado

So here is what happened- from my perspective- on May 8, 2024. South of Nashville. The emergency alert went off on my phone several times. Then some of my family members started texting and calling. I only received two messages before the cell towers were either slammed or went down. I pushed a recliner into the space that seemed safest in my house.

It is a little area where two bedroom doors and one bathroom door meet in a 5x5 area that opens into a living room with a high ceiling. It did not appear to be very safe but if everything caved in, they could find my body. I remember that even at the age of ten I was smart enough to know that we were not safe from a nuclear blast by hiding under our school desks and covering our faces. That position would just make us easier to identify.

That is how I felt on Wednesday. I should say that I believe that if the Lord wanted me alive then he would protect me, if he wanted to put me in storage and resurrect me at a later time, that would be fine also. I'm good either way. (As if I have any say in the matter.)

My two dogs, Ginny and Wyatt, paced back and forth and finally decided that sitting next to me was as safe as they were going to get. Very soon the sirens started. Fire, emergency, police, ambulance. A cacophony of disaster. The power went off. I was sitting in near darkness. The tornado touched down about half a mile from my house and ripped a trail of disaster several miles to within about half a mile of my grandson's house, several miles away. His wife, two children, one old dog and two puppies huddled in a practiced precision in the bathroom. My grandson told me later that his wife conducted herself in such a way that the children just thought that it was a false alarm like the other eight times they huddled in the bathroom. Good work, mom!

My neighborhood was immediately blocked off due to the houses that were destroyed, the trees being broken and uprooted and the live power lines that were down. One person lost their life. Another person was carried out. There was also a gravely injured horse. I stayed home so I did not actually see the devastation.

After the storm passed, I fixed a cold plate. Fortunately, I had purchased a family meal of Kentucky Fried Chicken (I could NOT believe the price!) the day before. I shared some with my daughter and had plenty left in the refrigerator. My dinner consisted of a piece of cold chicken, a hardboiled egg and a small grapefruit. It was a very nice "after the tornado" repast.

I was dining on the back porch with the dogs. They were sitting at attention, hoping that I would share. The dogs soon got excited and started barking at the front door. About that time, I heard, "Sheriff's Department!" and a rapping sound and saw a flashlight being shone into my house.

I opened the door, blocking the dogs, and greeted my guests in a long cotton gown. I had gotten ready for bed. They announced that they were there for a welfare check. I told them that I was fine and that I was eating dinner on the back porch with my dogs. Behind them was one of my neighbors who saw the emergency vehicle and came to see if he could help. God bless them all.

I thanked them and they stepped off the porch as I closed the door. They were prepared for an emergency. My neighbor later told me that they all had a good chuckle over my response that I was eating dinner on my back porch. I will send them a thank you note.

My daughters and grandson did not request the check. I think that my grandson, who was on a special task force of swift water rescue in Texas, might have mentioned to his chief that he could not get hold of me and the chief then requested that the Sheriff's Department come check on me. I surmise this. I don't know for sure. Good chief, taking care of the concerns of his men, if that was the case.

Someone asked me if I was afraid. No, not really. Between my childhood and marriage, my store of adrenaline is pretty much used up. I wasn't even annoyed. I don't like sitting in the dark. My mind races to places I would rather not go. I tried to think creative thoughts and remember the words to old songs. I needed to exercise my memory. I had a candle burning. If I had thought more about it, I would have gotten a pencil and paper and started writing. That would have been a more constructive use of my time than just sitting in the dark looking at the candle flame. Waiting.

I am sorry that anyone was alarmed for my safety because the phone service was down. Of course, no one knew that at the moment. They were only concerned that they could not get hold of a 78-year-old woman. I was fine. God bless all the emergency workers who risked their lives and worked to save people in the terrible rain and electrical storm that followed the tornado and those who worked to mitigate the destruction. And all the utility people who toiled through the storm to get things back to normal. Everything in my freezer was fine even though the power was out for about 26 hours. The ice cream was soft but, Meh. I like milkshakes. I am writing this on Saturday. The Internet Service has been down for three days, so far.

And bless all of those, including my grandson, who would rather have been home but "stayed the course" to help all of those in the flooded-out areas in Texas. And YES, contrary to popular belief, there are alligators in Texas. My question is- Why aren't we using them on the border?

Chapter 25
Goldenrod and Cows

Goldenrod. It is a bushy plant that grows about two to four feet tall and produces clusters of tiny yellow flowers. The poisonous substance in rayless goldenrod is tremetol, an alcohol that is present throughout the plant in both green and dry material. Tremetol is toxic to all livestock, and produces a condition known as "trembles." Young animals and humans can be poisoned by drinking milk from animals that have been feeding on rayless goldenrod. The odd thing about goldenrod is that it is mostly poisonous in alkali or gypsum soils. It is my understanding that it is not poisonous to cattle in other places. I ran cattle in New Mexico which is known for its alkali and gypsum soil.

My older cows would not eat goldenrod because they knew better. They taught their calves to avoid it. It does not taste good, and cattle will usually avoid it if there is anything else to eat. Of course, I kept them well fed enough that it was not a big danger for them. I was sharing a pasture with Billy one fall. He had purchased his cows from somewhere else, so they did not know about this toxic weed. I told him that he needed to move his cattle in the fall. He did not remove them soon enough, so they started dying. It is a slow death, and the cows get crazy before they die.

He finally asked me to help him gather his cows. We penned all but one and rode the pastures looking for the last one. Billy rode down into the river and found her. He succeeded in driving her up the embankment. He hollered at me that she was headed my way. The cow ran straight at me and kept charging my mare, even bending my foot up under the horse. She did not have horns, so she was not doing much damage to us. Thinking that I could get April, my mare, to knock the cow down, I kneed her and reined her to push on the cow. She was a roping horse and had never been called on to knock down a cow. She might have been thinking, "How close do we have to get before you drop a rope on her?"

The cow kept charging. Billy showed up and since I was the object of her anger, I told him to go ahead and open the pasture gate and I would fight her to the trailer.

When we got her to the trailer, which we had parked close to the fence, he closed the pasture gate behind her. The plan was to use the pasture fence and trailer gate as an alley to crowd her into the trailer. She kept fighting us, so Billy suggested that I climb up to the top of the fork of the gooseneck trailer. Billy had the bright idea that since she was mad at me, I should get down on the top rail at the front of the trailer so she could see me and charge. I did this. He was right.

He was crowding her closer to the trailer. She bellowed when she looked up and saw me, then she charged. Seeking to attack again, she finally jumped in. I did not think that Billy dismounted quickly enough to close the trailer gate, so I scrambled to jump down to close the gate and fell through the fork of the trailer. He must have gotten the trailer gate closed on her. I did not see that.

When I came to, I was lying face up under the bed of the pickup. I rolled over and crawled out from under the truck bed. Heaving, barely able to breathe, I got to my hands and knees. I was too weak to stand. My chest hurt and I was making a horrible sound as I tried to suck in oxygen. Benny kept asking me if I was ok, but I couldn't speak. Every bit of air had been knocked out of me. Everything was dark blue, and I saw stars. My chest felt like it was caved in. I could hear Billy asking me over and over if I was ok. I nodded but the horrible sounds I was making did not reassure him. A horrible growling, sucking sound. At first, I didn't realize that they were coming from me. All I could think was -bears.

After several minutes, I was able to crawl headfirst into the passenger's side of his pickup. My chest hurt and I still could not speak. I then wondered if I had collapsed my lungs. I don't know if you can reinflate them yourself. I finally got over it and could breathe normally.

He left the cow lying in the pen for several days while he moved the other cows. I told him that he needed to put her down. He finally did. Sometimes bad things happen to good cows.

Chapter 26
Another Mad Cow

There was another time Billy asked me to keep an eye on his cows while he was out of town. They were on hay fields. I agreed, so every morning, before I went to work, I checked on them. I was dressed up in nice slacks and in two-inch heels. Not really dressed for cow work, but I had promised to check on his cows, so I did.

One morning I pulled up to the field and counted. One was missing. I started driving around the farm and spotted the missing big red cow standing alone in a plowed field. There is nothing to eat there. I saw that she was in trouble, so I got out of the pickup and started walking across the plowed field toward her. She was lying down and getting up, changing sides and lying down again. As I got close to her, I could see why she was getting up and down continually. She had a calf hung up. The head was flopping up and down. I knew that it was dead. It had tried to come out headfirst instead of feet first. She saw me and started across the field towards me, running as fast as she could.

Apparently, she had decided that I was the reason for her distress. As she loomed closer and closer (her head seemed to be about 3 feet wide from my perspective) I had very little time to decide what to do. There were no rocks, and the dirt clods did not offer any protection. I waited until she was about 10 feet from me and then I threw up my arms and yelled. She veered off to the left and I quickly ran to my pickup and left the immediate area.

I called a couple of guys who knew Billy and they agreed to pen the cow and take care of the problem. I waited until they got to the farm and directed them to the cow. I stood behind the trailer as they pushed her toward the pen. There was no need for me to distress her more. I was only there to show them where she was and help as needed. They got her loaded and penned and later pulled the dead calf. Then I went to work.

A few months later, when we gathered the cows at Billy's place, I was told to cover an area so the cows would not get by the gate. I positioned my horse to cover the area. When that same cow saw me, she lowered her head and bellowed. I urged my horse a step closer, and she turned and went into the pen. Apparently being horseback made me too big a target. The next day I went to help Billy brand the calves that the men could not handle. His brother had helped him with the small, easy ones. That same crazy cow was in the pen. Billy and I were standing on the railing of the fence when she saw me and charged the fence. We jumped back and left her alone. Apparently, cows hold grudges.

Chapter 27
The Black Panther

Anyone who knows me knows that I don't tell tall tales. The facts are usually enough to make the stories interesting. I was ranging my cattle on a piece of land that the Pecos River ran through. The banks of the river were covered with salt cedar trees (also known as Tamarisk), cattails and dried tumbleweeds. It forms a dense thicket.

I was going down to the river to check on the cattle one Saturday. Pigner said that he wanted to go with me. Since I had to drive through Pigner's property to get to my pasture, I couldn't very well refuse. He and his family hunted and fished in the river, and he wanted to look for good spots. He wedged himself into my Toyota Diesel pickup and his twelve-year-old grandson, Marlon, hopped into the bed of the truck and stood up, holding the edge of the cab.

I checked the fences. They were up and I did not find the cattle. I then started driving along the river, craning my neck at every curve to see as far ahead as I could and looking across the river as the cattle tended to cross to the other side. Pigner was looking out the passenger side window, off to the right when there was an explosion of black across the front of my truck.

A shiny, black panther (sometimes called a mountain lion, puma or cougar) was lying on the side of the dirt road we were traveling. He or she leapt right across the road in front of the truck. From nose to tail it stretched the width of the pickup. That would have been about six feet. A small, chiseled head, a long, glistening body and tail. A beautiful sight and gone in a minute.

For just a moment I wondered if I had really seen it. Then Marlon started pounding on the roof of the cab yelling, "Did you see it?! Did you see it?!" Pigner had missed it, "What? What?" I yelled, "I saw it!"

I stopped the truck, and we got out to try and track it. We saw where it lay, and paw prints on both sides of the road. None on the road, which tells you how far it jumped. We did not find any tracks through the trees. It only occurred to me, some thirty-five years later, that we should have looked up. It might have been IN the trees. DUH!

When I got to work on Monday, I told the guys what I had seen. They did not believe me. They guffawed at my story, since none of them had ever heard of a black panther on the Pecos River.

Benny went home that night and told the tale to an old man who grew up along the river. The old man assured him that when he was young there were many black panthers along with the normal tan colored ones on the river. He told Benny that they roamed up and down the rivers from Mexico to northern New Mexico.

The old man validated my claim, but many others refused to believe such a tale. I wish I had a picture of that big, black cat that morning. It must have moved along because I did not lose any cattle to the hunter. I never dehorned my cows. That would have disarmed them. It must be said that my cattle always grazed close together and moved in a tight bunch. They never spread out to graze the way cattle normally do. They sensed the danger and protected themselves.

Chapter 28
The Sewer Line

I had a tenant who was on HUD. This is also referred to as Section Eight Housing. This is a government program which provides for families that can't afford decent shelter. I named the tenant Mack, as in Mack the Knife. She was in violation of her Lease Agreement because she did not have the electricity or gas turned on. When CYFD, (Children, Youth and Family Department), called on her to check on the children's welfare, the inspector did not notice that the family was eating sandwiches in the dark. I called and reported this to the agency. I don't know if they did anything about it.

We have a legal responsibility to report child or elder abuse. Even if we did not, I believe we all have a moral responsibility to do this.

Mack was in jail for stabbing her husband. They had been arguing. He called her a name and she grabbed a steak knife and stabbed him. He called the police. A non-threatening wound, but she went to jail. She was pregnant at the time.

Since Mack was in jail, I let the grandmother stay in the house to care for the children. When she did not pay the rent as per our written agreement, (not a rental agreement), and I attempted to evict her (based on the rental agreement that I had with Mack), the deputy would not enforce the eviction notice from the court because Mack was in jail, (not in the house), and there were three minors in the house. I had to file in court against the grandmother to get the eviction. This caused another delay in the eviction of these people.

These tenants apparently did not want me around (they owed me rent), so when the sewer line backed up, they took the cap off the sewer clean-out, letting the sewage run out onto the ground. They stacked empty boxes and broken furniture around the pool of sewage so I would not notice. I filed a Notice of Failure to Pay Rent.

I did a drive-by early on the morning we were due in court. I drove in front of the house and behind. Mack was in jail for stabbing her husband, so her mother showed up. Mother had called Code Enforcement that morning and reported that I refused to fix the sewer line. She then reported this to the judge while we were in court. He asked me if I knew about this, and I replied that I had driven by that morning and saw boxes and furniture piled over the clean-out. He dismissed her charge against me.

By the time I finally got the Eviction Order from the court, Mack, her husband, the grandmother, and three children were all living in the house. YEP! The felony against Mack was dismissed because the police had failed to gather the alleged weapon when they arrested her. No weapon, no evidence, therefore no crime. AND all was apparently forgiven in the love nest.

The husband had recently gotten out of prison, so he had nowhere else to go. Besides, he proved handy to her for the southern engineering of the water lines and some other nefarious schemes.

Prior to this, the Water Department had sent me a letter threatening to tear up my water lines if I did not take action against the tenant. I am not sure that this is even legal. I don't think they can go on private property and tear up privately owned lines. The Water Department had turned off the water. The tenant turned it back on. The Water Department then slugged the line. The tenant managed to bypass the plug. The Water Company then removed the meter. Next, the tenant ran a line from a neighbor's property. This is illegal.

Note: I have an even more horrific story of what they did to the gas line, but that is a story for another time.

Rather than contest the proposed action of the Water Department, I responded to the letter by calling and explaining my legal problems. I assured the Water Department that I was actively involved in getting the deadbeats out of my house. I don't take kindly to being threatened but I did understand their dilemma. I just did not like them thrusting their problem on me or threatening me. Sometimes it is easier to go with the flow than stand your ground on things like this. Choose which hill you want to defend. I was going to have to resolve this issue, regardless.

Later, when I got the house back, I found that the reason the sewer backed up was because the children had dropped water balloons down one of the clean-outs, effectively blocking the sewage from flowing properly. This house had two clean-outs because the bathrooms were on the opposite ends of the house. This was the cause of the sewer backup. Stupid is as stupid does.

Postscript: When I first rented to Mack, she had just gotten out of jail for larceny. To get her children back, she had to have a house for them. I let her rent one, even though she got so excited when I told her that she backed into my pickup, denting my bumper. I also wrote her resume and printed out copies, made her some business cards, paid for a mechanic to look at her car, purchased a battery for said car, took her oldest to Walmart to purchase all his school supplies and did many other things to help her get on her feet. NO good deed goes unpunished.

Chapter 29
The Dirty Deputy

I got home late one night after working on a rental. The door opened without a key. The first thing I noticed was that part of the door lock was on the floor. The second thing was an empty bottle of bourbon on the kitchen floor. A television and a VCR were missing. A large toolbox full of tools was gone. I called the Sheriff's Department and cleaned up the mess. While I waited, I decided to fix dinner. The package of meat was not in the refrigerator. I looked everywhere, even under the sofa. I thought that perhaps I had left it on the counter and the cat had gotten it. No. It was missing. Thankfully the thieves had not found my guns, nor had they taken my computer and saddle.

I later figured out that it was because there were four people in the car, and they did not have room for a computer and a saddle. The main thief and his wife came by the next day to pick up what they had missed. Fortunately, I was there talking to a deputy. But that is another story.

Deputy Hector showed up and I let him in the house. He sat down on the sofa and looked around. In all my dealings with the law I have never had anyone look around and assess things while they were making a report. Taking the report seemed secondary to him. It was more like he was casing the place. He said, "This is a nice house. Nice things. I have always wanted a place like this."

I ignored the remark and started enumerating the missing items. When he asked if there was anything else, like money, I remembered the stash I had in the freezer. I said, "Yes, I have money in the freezer." I got up to check and he was hot on my heels. When I pulled the envelope out, I said, "Well, they didn't find this." I reached to put it back and he quickly took it out of my hands, and asked me, "How much is in here?" I answered, "About three hundred dollars." He counted it and said, "There is three hundred and sixty dollars here." I took it from him and as I put it back in the freezer I said, "They must have put some in for all of the things that they stole."

We stood in the kitchen while he looked around. Noticing that the back door was nailed shut, he commented, "So, you nailed the door shut." I replied, "Yes, I guess if anyone breaks in, I will have to shoot my way out." New Mexico is not a stand your ground state. You are only allowed to shoot in self-defense, otherwise you must flee. By this time, I knew that we were playing some kind of game. I wanted him out of my house.

He continued to stand in the kitchen, so I walked outside, stating, "Well, I guess you have everything you need." Before he walked to his car, he shone his flashlight across my pickup and said, "Green Dodge Dakota pickup. If I see that on the road, I'll wave at you." He seemed to be committing everything to memory. It made me very nervous.

The next day I called a relative in the Sheriff's Department. I explained about the break-in and the subsequent visit by the deputy. He listened to the whole story and then said, "Okay, we are taking care of it." I thought that was an odd turn of phrase, but it turned out not to be.

Here is the rest of the story: Hector had been patrolling in the countryside. There was a bar in the middle of nowhere which the farm hands frequented. Hector would stop them after they left the bar and demand all their money on threat of arrest. Word about this got back to the Sheriff's Department, and they set up a sting operation.

Here is how the sting went down. One night a call came in to the dispatcher from a deputy, saying that he had stopped a drunk and was taking him to jail. The officer said he needed someone to come and stay with the car until he could get back from the jail to finish up the inspection. A call went out to Hector. The car had been rigged with cameras and several hundred dollars had been dusted with tracing powder. Hector showed up and soon started searching through the car.

When he discovered the money stashed in the glove box, he first put it inside his shirt. Time passed. He was becoming increasingly anxious and soon called the dispatcher, wanting to know how much longer he needed to remain with the car. She assured him that the arresting officer was on his way. As Hector waited, he changed his mind and put the money in his thermos, in the trunk of his car. The arresting officers showed up, found the money, and Hector was arrested. He spent three years in jail.

I did not get my belongings back, but I was glad that the dirty deputy was off the street. People like him give law officers a bad name.

Chapter 30
Lolli's Story

Officers can enforce any part of a criminal law, but they are not supposed to get involved in civil law. Individuals can get in trouble if they try to stand up for their rights. The law officers have very wide discretion. On that note, this next story is best told as a play because of all the actors involved.

Here are the players in this little episode:

Lolli- The Little Old Landlady
CPO- City Police Officer
DT- Dying Tenant
CC- Coward of the County, a friend of DT.

CC called Lolli and said that DT was dying and that he (CC), and DT's daughters were cleaning out DT's house. DT was in the hospital and not expected to live. CC called Lolli after he and DT's girlfriend had removed most of the valuable things. When Lolli arrived at the house she noticed that the den, which had been converted into a workroom, was devoid of all tools. The external electrical system and workbench, which DT had installed, had been ripped from the walls. All the kitchen cupboards had been emptied, and the kitchen appliances were missing, as was some of the furniture. All the closets were empty.

DT's girlfriend and CC were loading things into their cars and claiming rights to things in the house. CC offered to sell some of the furniture to Lolli and she refused, stating that DT already owed her a month's rent and from the looks of the house, also several thousand dollars in damages. Then CC offered her a few things in return for the past due rent. Lolli accepted and wrote a letter stating the agreement. She also asked that an inventory be made of everything that had been or was being removed from the premises.

This is a legal requirement in New Mexico and required of all landlords. This was not done. CC was overheard instructing the movers to deliver some items to a third party. DT's daughters told Lolli that CC had the authority to store or dispose of everything in the house. CC and DT's girlfriend promised to leave the house ready for the next tenant to rent by the first of the month. This did not happen.

DT did not die. Several weeks after he got out of the hospital, he started going through one of his storage units. When he could not find some kitchen appliances and other things, he confronted CC.

CC, coward that he is, said that Lolli must have taken them. DT then went to the Police Department. DT complained to CPO, who is the city police officer, in case you are having trouble keeping track of the players in this little drama. CPO called Lolli, threatening her, refusing to identify himself by first name or badge number (three times), and refusing to listen to any explanation of the situation and the laws that apply. This was a civil matter, not criminal. CPO hung up on Lolli.

An hour later someone from the Sheriff's Office called and she explained everything to the deputy. He replied that he figured it was something like that and thanked her for her time. She thought that was the end of the situation.

Lolli wrote a letter of complaint to the mayor about the unprofessional conduct, lack of knowledge of Landlord/ Tenant law and the failure of CPO to identify himself by first name or badge number.

Six weeks later, CPO showed up at Lolli's house with three other officers, called Lolli, and said, "You need to get to your house. Right Now! I have a warrant for your arrest. If you do not get up here immediately, I will kick in the door!" Lolli told him that he better not damage her house. CPO then called a locksmith.

She showed up at her house and was arrested for fourth-degree larceny and taken to jail. She was released on her own recognizance. Lolli immediately contacted her attorney and he explained to her that the value of items contested had to be above five hundred dollars for there to be a charge of Fourth Degree Larceny.

Although DT placed a value of four hundred and seventy-five dollars on the contested items, the District Attorney's office agreed to prosecute for 4th-degree larceny which is described as being more than five hundred but less than twenty-five hundred and one dollars. Did you catch that?

SOOOO—-CPO had now involved a judge, four law officers, four squad cars, a locksmith, the District Attorney's office, and court personnel for an illegal arrest.

Lolli's attorney cleared her name. She could have received eighteen months in jail and a five thousand dollar fine, had she been prosecuted as charged. No doubt the mayor passed the letter to CPO's superior, the Chief of Police. CPO, while seething in court about the outcome of the case, at least had the satisfaction of paying Lolli back for the letter that she had written to the mayor. Such a letter would be entered into CPO's employment record, thus putting a black mark in his personnel file. No wonder he arrested Lolli.

Postscript to this—Lolli later had a friend check to see what the outcome was for the law officer. Apparently, he was put on suspension and quit the force, moving out of state.

"Nothing in the world can take the place of persistence. Talent will not; nothing is more common than unsuccessful people with talent. Genius will not; unrewarded genius is almost a proverb. Education will not; the world is full of educated derelicts. Persistence and determination alone are omnipotent. The slogan 'press on' has solved and always will solve the problems of the human race."

~*Calvin Coolidge, the thirtieth President of the United States.*

About the Author

After spending her youth on the sunny beaches of Southern California, Sandra moved to New Mexico where she finished her education and began her working career in Interior Design. This enabled her to pursue her real love -Ranching. She spent over twenty years raising cattle and children. Left alone to do both, she rapidly grew in experience from both of these ventures.

With the children gone and the cattle sold, she was able to purchase many abused and neglected houses. She spent her daylight hours in the field of interior design and ultimately purchased many houses in a little over six years. She remodeled, repaired, and refurbished these homes on evenings and weekends, turning them into rentals. She spent twenty-five years working and managing her rentals in her off hours.

Sandra uses humor and a unique insight into the human condition to explain the day-to-day events which she encountered in her three very different endeavors.

She spent 58 years in New Mexico before retiring to Middle Tennessee where she enjoys family, friends and gardening. She still spends her free time writing. Her first book, The Other Side Of The River: A Story Of Love, War, Cattle And Cowboys was published in February 2023. It is an historical fiction account of ranching in two different eras. Her second book, The Rental Roller Coaster: The Ups And Downs Of A Successful Landlord, was published in October 2023. It is a true account of dilemmas and practical solutions to some of the many problems encountered by landlords. It is written with her unique wit and perspective.

Her third book, which you hold in your hands, is a compilation of some of her experiences after her children were raised. From repossessing a car, to witches, to black panthers, every story is true and unadorned.

Her next is a children's story and coloring book. Look for it later this year.

www.ingramcontent.com/pod-product-compliance
Lightning Source LLC
Chambersburg PA
CBHW060408050426
42449CB00009B/1934